THE
WIVENHO

AND

BRIGHTLINGSEA
RAILWAY

Paul Brown

IAN HENRY PUBLICATIONS

First published 1985
Reprinted 1986
Revised edition 1995

© Paul Brown, 1985, 1995

ISBN 0 86025 456 9

British Library Cataloguing in Publication Data

Brown, Paul
    Wivenhoe & Brightlingsea Railway.
    1. Wivenhoe & Brightlingsea Railway. 2. Railroads--England--Wivenhoe region
(Essex)--Branch lines.
    I. Title.
    385'.09426'72   HE3020.W5

Printed by
Halstan & Co., Ltd., Plantation Road, Amersham, Buckinghamshire HP6 6HJ
for
Ian Henry Publications, Ltd.
20 Park Drive, Romford, Essex RM1 4LH

INTRODUCTION

This is the story of a piece of land five miles long and five feet wide over the period of one hundred years - a railway crossing a section of deserted marshland between the small Essex towns of Wivenhoe and Brightlingsea.

Its life and its story come from two sources. It was built, firstly, to shield the marshes from the river and the sea, a sea that must be remembered, not for summer days on the beach, but the days when wind makes speech impossible, tears flow from the eyes with the cold, and driving spray fills the air; and, secondly, for the people who are the life of any railway - Victorian speculators, working men who toiled long hours for little pay, those who died because the railway had been built, and the soldiers of two world wars for whom a railway journey was to be the last memory of England.

After twenty years of dealing with the 'old line', I have gained so much information, especially maps and photographs, that I have decided to make it all into this definitive book.

The text remains almost the same as earlier editions - as does the dedication:

To the old men of the railway, those who knew, who told me, and are no more.

Sprats being unloaded on Brightlingsea Hard in the 1920's

One road in, one road out. An early map of
Brightlingsea showing the road in from Thorrington
and the curve of the marsh that was to have a
railway.

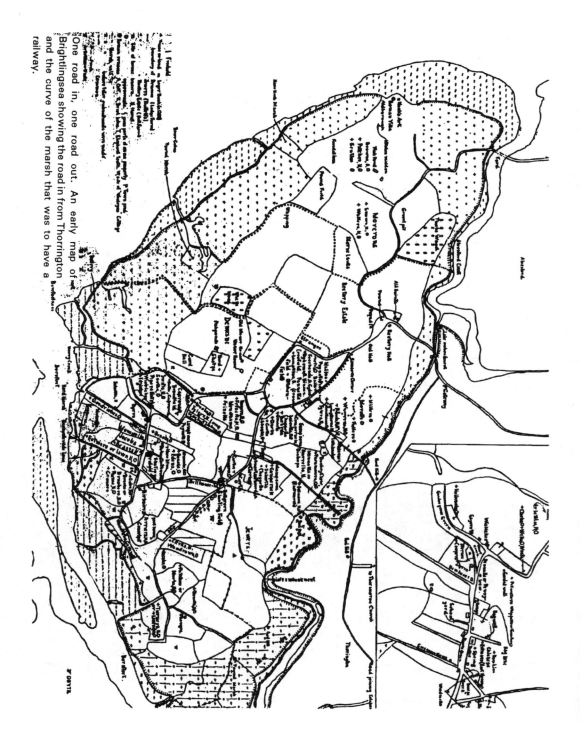

THE NORTHERN LORDS

"They have the money, I have the brains", was the way George Bradley put it. His brains now told him that, along with two financiers, he should buy up the Lordship of the Manor of Brightlingsea, not just for the usual purpose of re-selling it later for a profit, but here was a new venture to be tried: why not build a railway across a stretch of wild marsh-land between Brightlingsea and Wivenhoe, neighbouring towns on the River Colne?

The Lordship was bought from John Dorian Magens who, having no heirs or successors, signed away the rights that had been brought into his family by Nicolas Magens almost a hundred years before. The rights fell into the hands of three men - not the locals one would suppose (for Brightlingsea was an isolated settlement of north-east Essex with a single road leading into the town: so isolated was it that a local saying was "As sure as the Devil's in Bentley", referring to a village all of five miles distant), but from an area termed 'North of Ipswich' - two from Yorkshire and one from the Midlands.

Born in Boston, Bradley, then aged 35, had moved to Castleford, Yorkshire, some nine years previously. He was a solicitor, glassworks owner and, above all, a great organiser where money was involved. Buying up Manor rights was

his speciality: he already had five in his native Lincolnshire, as well as others in Suffolk, Somerset, Hampshire and Yorkshire, his boast of his then-residence being "You might say that I made Castleford". It seemed to him that the future was a choice between becoming a solicitor for neighbouring Pontefract or speculating on any thing that looked like paying a profit.

He needed a friend to supervise the financial side and found one in James Robinson, a banker, who lived at Pontefract and was often concerned with Bradley in land transactions, including the purchase of manorial rights.

Someone then had to put up the money and the man they found was not living nearby, but at Stourbridge in Warwickshire. His name was Edward Westwood, a manufacturer of glass and stoneware bottles and, possibly, a malster. What connection he could have had with the two Yorkshiremen is un-known, unless an advertisement in some dusty newspaper can provide the link, as there was certainly no association between them by trade or residence.

So, there they were - Bradley had the brains and know-how, Robinson handled the money, Westwood gave the finance. Why, though, the idea of building a railway? Agreed, everybody was doing it and, possibly, George Bradley was trying for a new speculation. He might have had contact with George Hudson, the 'Railway King' of York, who, some 15 years earlier had been made Chairman of the Eastern Counties Railway, until the start of his fall from public favour some four years later. Bradley had seemed, at the time of the purchase, to be more interested in coal mining and the profits that that might give.

The attraction of building a railway, however, was easy to understand. Although local legend still talks of it as having been made as a cheap and easy way to get a sea wall to protect their property, the real answer lies in one word - sprats! At the time this plentiful fish was used only as manure by the local farmers. A similar reason had led, in 1845, to the project for building a railway from Colchester to Harwich. The company hoping to build it called themselves the Harwich and Colchester Railway and Pier Company, the plan being that a line should run from Castle Yard, just in front of Colchester Castle, round the Castle down the slope and out towards Elmstead Market. From there a branch was to run to a pier on a spit of land to the north of Alresford Creek. It seems that the motive, aided by the mention of the building of 'warehouses, wharves and landing places', was to transport the sprats from Alresford Creek to Harwich for shipping to the continent. The engineers for the line, Gibbs and Paine, had already been chosen, but, like so many other railway speculations of the

Sprats being unloaded on to the fields for manure and free food for the seabirds. (*Photo Douglas Went*)

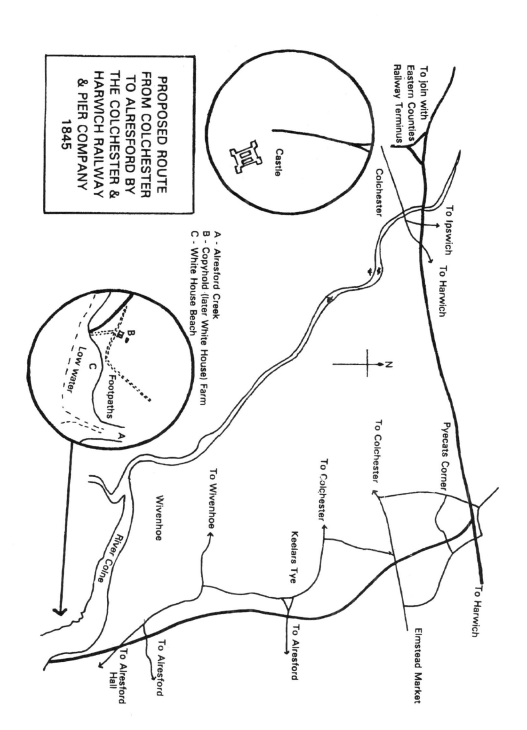

PROPOSED ROUTE
FROM COLCHESTER
TO ALRESFORD BY
THE COLCHESTER &
HARWICH RAILWAY
& PIER COMPANY
1845

A - Alresford Creek
B - Copyhold (later White House) Farm
C - White House Beach

To join with
Eastern Counties
Railway Terminus

Castle

Colchester

To Ipswich

To Harwich

Pyecats Corner

To Colchester

To Colchester

Elmstead Market

To Harwich

Keelars Tye

To Alresford

N

Low water

Footpaths

B

C

A

Wivenhoe

To Wivenhoe

River Colne

To Alresford
Hall

To Alresford

5

day, it came to nothing. The local papers were full of schemes for railways that were never constructed - and accounts of morbid accidents on those that were.

The new Lords of the Manor knew that time was short to get their railway started, as they had a rival, the Tendring Hundred Railway Company, formed a year earlier in 1859, who were planning to extend to Wivenhoe the already constructed line to Colchester, Hythe.

This new development followed a lull in railway building in this corner of Essex: perhaps the fall from grace of George Hudson had made speculators think twice. On 28th March, 1843, the Eastern Counties Railway completed a rail link between London and Colchester and, on 15th June, 1846, the Eastern Union Railway Company opened its line from Colchester to Ipswich, in pursuit of the Eastern Counties' aim of reaching Norwich, achieved three years later. In the cut and thrust world of Victorian railway speculation, the Eastern Counties finally won control of the area by taking over the Eastern Union in 1854.

In 1847, one year after the opening of the Colchester-Ipswich line, the Stour Valley Railway completed the 'off-shoot' from Colchester to Hythe Quay to allow access to Colchester Docks. The next development came 16 years later, when the Tendring Hundred Railway opened a line to Wivenhoe which had been approved in 1860, as the three speculators knew only too well. They needed to obtain an Act of Parliament quickly before the Tendring Company beat them to it, for the Tendring Hundred

Railway Company was a formidable opponent and they, too, realised that a line to Brightlingsea would be profitable.

The Tendring Company's directors were determined men too. John Cobbold, M.P., was one of the family of brewers and bankers, who had been involved in East Anglian railways since 1841, only 12 years after Stephenson's *Rocket* had made its historic run. Another was Sir Claude de Crespigny, a baronet and speculator in any enterprise with promise of reward. In 1860, at the age of 42, he was the father of 4 sons and 7 daughters and Colonel of the First Battalion, Essex Regiment.

Not much time could be lost if this company was to be beaten by George Bradley and his associates. Firstly, the land needed to build a railway had to be bought. The proposed land on the Brightlingsea side of Alresford Creek was already under the control of the new Lords of the Manor, but some legal difficulties had to be eliminated, resulting in a strange auction taking place on 22nd February, 1861, in the *Three Cups Hotel,* Colchester. All the farming land and property on the north side of the River Colne estuary was split up into seven lots to be sold. George Bradley, giving his address as 'A Solicitor of Castleford in Yorkshire', was one who could be contacted beforehand for plans of the land to be auctioned. In fact, the three new Lords were rarely seen in Brightlingsea, leaving their affairs in the hands of a local agent, Mr Nathaniel Cobb.

The auction was unusual, in that all the lots put up failed to reach their

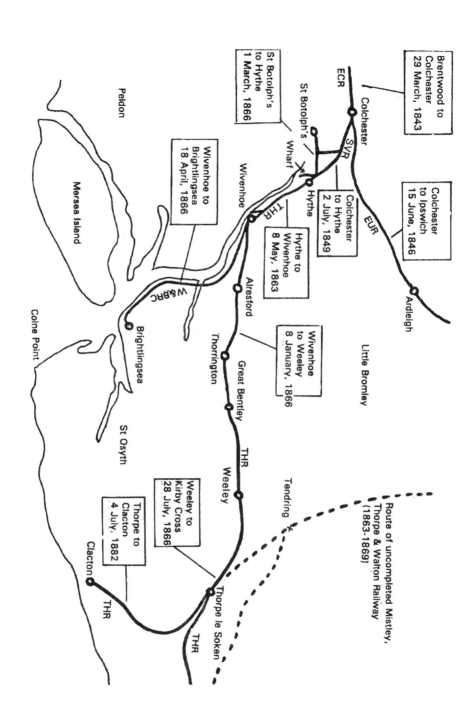

Brentwood to
Colchester
29 March, 1843

St Botolph's
to Hythe
1 March, 1866

Wivenhoe to
Brightlingsea
18 April, 1866

Colchester
to Hythe
2 July, 1849

Hythe to
Wivenhoe
8 May, 1863

Wivenhoe
to Weeley
8 January, 1866

Weeley to
Kirby Cross
28 July, 1866

Thorpe to
Clacton
4 July, 1882

Colchester
to Ipswich
15 June, 1846

Route of uncompleted Mistley,
Thorpe & Walton Railway
(1863-1869)

Peldon

Mersea Island

Colne Point

Growth of Local Lines

Colchester

ECR

SVR

St Botolph's

Wharf

Wivenhoe

Hythe

THR

W&BRC

Alresford

Brightlingsea

Thorrington

Great Bentley

St Osyth

Weeley

THR

Tendring

Thorpe le Soken

THR

Clacton

THR

EUR

Little Bromley

Ardleigh

7

reserve price, although, as the local paper commented, "Bidding was very spirited up to a certain point". However, after the bidding was over it was disclosed that it had been decided to sell a small strip of land next to the marsh for the purpose of building a railway. The sum for which it was sold was never mentioned, if, in fact, it needed to be sold at all, for the Lords of the Manor would hardly sell their own property to themselves. It is also worth guessing who the spirited bidders were and how much they got paid afterwards!

Plans for Brightlingsea Branch, 1860 (9th November)

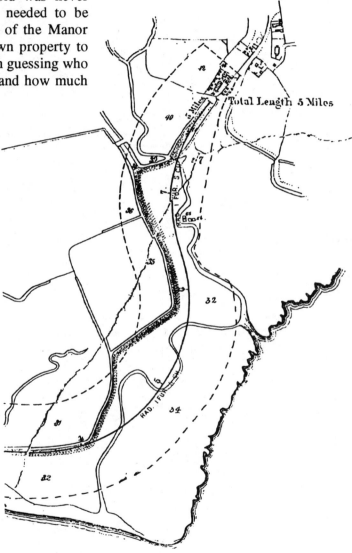

BRIGHTLINGSEA

Total Length 5 Miles

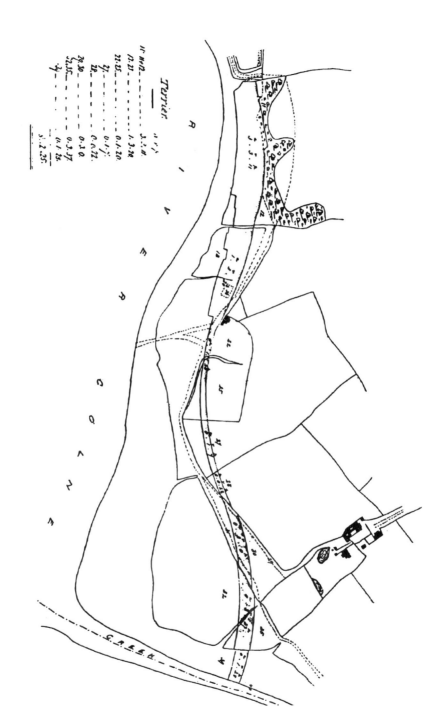

Harriet Higginbotham W & B.R.C. Sale, 1864

9

The land on one side of Alresford Creek was now obtained, but the stretch to Wivenhoe still needed to be acquired. Mary Higginbotham of London owned both the Manors of Alresford, a village two miles from Wivenhoe, and another local Manor, Cockaynes. On her death in 1839 she had left 'a third share in the Lands consisting of parts of Alresford, Lodge Farm, Lime Kiln Farm and Old Ballast Quay Farm ' - the land bordering the Wivenhoe side of Alresford Creek - to her sister, Harriet, who was living with a companion, Elizabeth Jones, in Brompton, Middlesex. Harriet eventually agreed with the other beneficiaries to sell the land for £650, but she had to wait until July, 1863, for her share of £216.13s.4d. She already was the owner of considerable land in the Wivenhoe area: her brother, George, was to live in Alresford and was to marry a local girl, Maria from Church Farm, so it must not be thought that the Higginbothams were absentee landlords, as in the case of the Brightlingsea Lords. Harriet was not to stay to see the opening of the railway, for she had sold all her property in the area by 1866.

The land having been bought, an Act of Parliament had to be obtained. It was about this time that Sir Claude de Crespigny was to resign from the Board of the Tendring Hundred Railway, due, as he put it, to military commitments.

The actual siting of the railway through Wivenhoe offered few problems. The Corsellis family, the usual occupiers of Wivenhoe Hall, were living for a while at Benson, Oxfordshire. The

Sir Claude Champion de Crespigny, the Line's first Chairman (*Courtesy of Major Grahame*)

person in residence at the Hall was Sir Claude, who had no objection to the railway skirting the Hall boundary, although a tree line was started to shield the Hall from the newcomer.

After passing under the High Street, the track was to cross an area of rough grassland until it came to Anglesea Road, which was only built to where the intended bridge ran under the road from the shipyards (Paget Road did not exist at this time). The only building that needed to be pulled down was a small house on the Anglesea Road belonging to Philip Sainty.

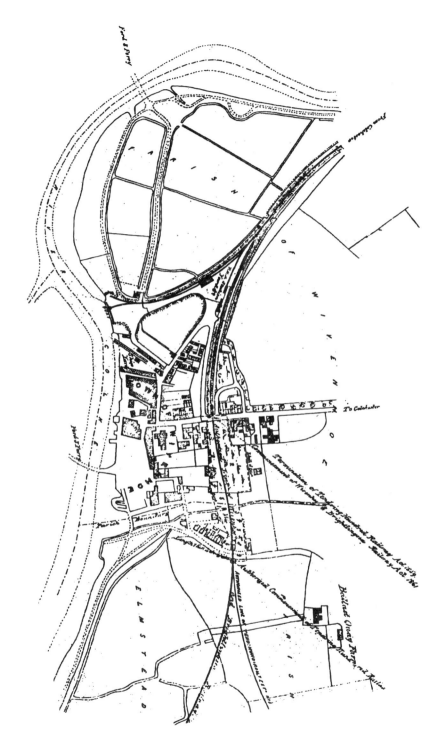

T. H. R. extension to Frinton and Walton,
November, 1863

11

Anglesea Road bridge, Wivenhoe, next to the branch off to Brightlingsea from the main line. A wall protects the footpath from horse and cart traffic. Photograph taken about 1910

On 11th July, 1861, the Act was passed by the House of Commons and the Wivenhoe and Brightlingsea Railway Company was officially formed. The directors of the Tendring Company were said to be very unhappy about this. They still hoped to gain permission to build a railway to Brightlingsea and even tried to do so after the W & B R C was formed. At a shareholders' meeting it was stated that, if the new company did not meet with success, they would build a line from Brightlingsea to Thorrington, branching off from their proposed route from Wivenhoe to Weeley *en route* to Walton. They had even tried to get permission to build the section from Wivenhoe to Great Bentley immediately, so that the Brightlingsea section could be

got under way as quickly as possible. Initially, though, they had been forced to withdraw their objection to the Wivenhoe and Brightlingsea Company on 1st May, 1861.

A quick look at the map will show the advantages of building a line across the firm ground from Thorrington, instead of skirting open marshland liable to flooding. There was, at that time, a man living in a barge in an area known for ever afterwards as 'Noah's Ark': the barge had been thrown up on to the marsh by a high tide years before. Now the W & B R C were planning to build a railway to run between the barge and the sea. It might, as has already been suggested, be an easy way for the Lords of the Manor to get a free sea wall as

well as a railway, but, if it was, this was a terrible mistake, as was to be demonstrated from time to time during the next hundred years.

There is a map in *the Essex Standard* of November, 1861, showing a proposed railway route from Brightlingsea to Alresford, via Thorrington, but this must have been the Tendring proposal, as, by then, the auction to obtain a riverside strip had taken place.

An 'Incorporation of Company Powers to make a Railway' notice had been put forward on 7th November, 1860, laying out the path for the new railway. It was to start from a garden belonging to William Jolliffe adjoining the road from Wivenhoe to Colchester and was to end at the sea wall in Brightlingsea, near a field called Weller's Marsh. The hoped-for Act would, it stated, amend the Tendring Hundred Railway Act of 1859. Things were now getting under way - and the Wivenhoe and Brightlingsea were winning.

Now came a blow to the Tendring company, which perhaps shows how wise it is to trust no-one in business dealings. Sir Claude de Crespigny had seemed very agreeable to the railway running round the property he was living in and he had, of course, recently resigned from the Tendring Hundred Railway. It came as no shock to those following Victorian speculation when the new Chairman of the W & B R C was announced as none

Where the railway was to run. Brightlingsea in 1800 - drawn by Len Lewes. It is interesting to compare all Mr Lewes's maps as they are to the same scale and provide a useful comparison.

14

other than - Sir Claude. After he had seen the way the Acts were going he had changed sides, for this company had got its Act of Parliament and seemed a much safer bet. Possibly his living at Wivenhoe Hall had enabled him to keep a close eye on the progress of both companies.

It is difficult when one visits Brightlingsea today to understand why he wanted to change, but it is as well to pause and examine the importance of Brightlingsea at that time in relation to other towns and villages in the area - it was, in fact, the largest town between Colchester and Harwich! Brightlingsea was an expanding town, the population having risen from 1,020 in 1811 to 2,557 in 1861, exclusive of some 400 fishermen and boys absent when the census was taken. Other local figures were - Alresford 248, Thorrington 424, Great Bentley 1,033, Weeley 630, Thorpe-le-Soken 697, Great Clacton [Clacton-on-Sea being non-existent] 1,208, while Frinton consisted of just 6 houses. St Osyth, with a population of 1,638, comes into the story a little later.

George Bradley was the Secretary to the Company, with James Robinson as Treasurer: they were to bring in another friend, Richard Moxon, as another Director. He was a client of George Bradley's, and already quite influential in Pontefract, where he was to be Mayor on several occasions. Being in the malting business it is quite possible that he looked upon Brightlingsea as a means of bringing East Anglian grain to within three miles of Pontefract by barge to further his business.

The powers to build a railway having been secured, things settled down for a while, during which period contractors had to be found and the problem of spanning the 150 yards of Alresford Creek had to be examined.

Wivenhoe, with a population of 1,843, was to get its railway on 8th May, 1863, when the Tendring Hundred line from Colchester Hythe was officially opened. One event marred the occasion. The day before the opening some local boys found a hand trolley and took it in turns to push it about on the lines of the goods sidings. A local man, Mr Holbrook, joined in, helping the lads to load it with metal and giving them rides on it. Before long this became an attraction for all the youngsters in the area and, sadly, 12 year old Emma Sainty, sitting on a corner of the trolley, fell off on her first trip, was run over and killed. Holbrook, seeing what happened, ran off, but later gave evidence at the inquest.

Wivenhoe used to be the port for Colchester when cargoes from vessels that could not navigate the Colne any higher were trans-shipped to lighters to complete their journey. The difficulties of this, together with the coming of the railway to Colchester from London and Ipswich, steadily diminished Wivenhoe's importance as a port, and declined further following the deepening of the Colne as far as the Hythe in 1854.

As with Brightlingsea, the possibility of landing sprats at Wivenhoe had been considered. No longer should the fields be filled with fish manure - there was the

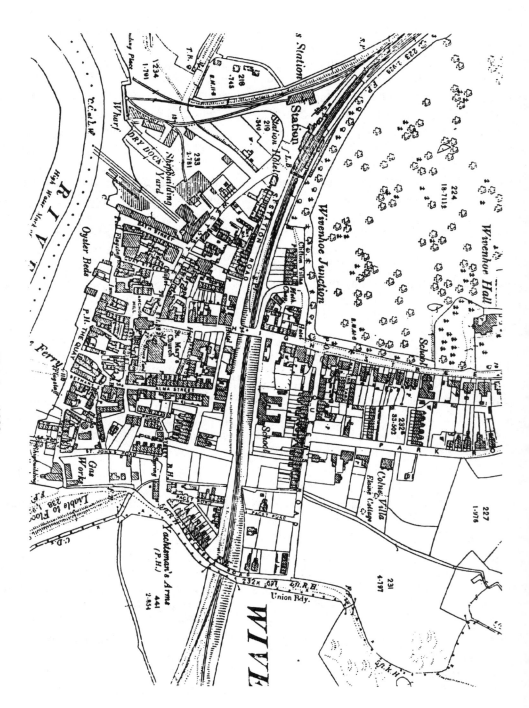

Wivenhoe, 1893

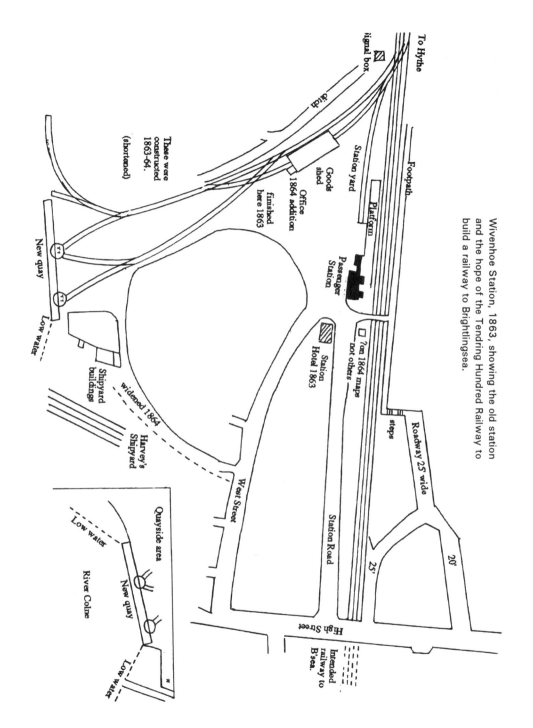

Wivenhoe Station, 1863, showing the old station and the hope of the Tendring Hundred Railway to build a railway to Brightlingsea.

To Hythe

signal box

ditch

Station yard

Goods shed

Office 1864 addition finished here 1863

These were constructed 1863-64. (shortened)

New quay

Low water

Shipyard buildings

Harvey's Shipyard

widened 1864

Platform

Footpath

Passenger Station

Station Hotel 1863

? on 1864 maps not others

steps

Roadway 25' wide

25'

20'

West Street

Station Road

High Street

Intended railway to B'sea.

Quayside area

Low water

New quay

River Colne

Low water

*

Wivenhoe and the Colne Estuary before the railway came
to Brightlingsea (*Print dated 1832*)

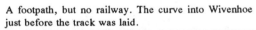

A footpath, but no railway. The curve into Wivenhoe
just before the track was laid.

London market to capture - but there were problems, the main difficulty being that boats had to wait for the tide before they could get alongside the Quay to unload on to trucks which were then pulled by horses to the station. This was doubly inconvenient because the sprats could only be unloaded twice a day and the varying times of the tide necessitated working at odd hours. Brightlingsea, as the Tendring Hundred Company well knew, could solve the difficulty.

The new Wivenhoe station was close to John Harvey's shipyard, where his reputation as a designer of fast schooners was at its height. The Goods Yard was to be completed in the following year to reach the new quay - 'Railway Quay', as it was called by the locals, with two turntables on the quayside to serve the sprat boats. The simple goods shed quickly gained an office and stables were added, where not only the carter's horses could be kept, but also those of the company. Two horses were to be stabled there until well into the steam locomotive age. These, like the engines on the line, were part of the Great Eastern Railway Company, which had come into being in July, 1862, and began the practice of buying large shares in any smaller company's enterprises - 70% in the case of the Tendring Hundred Railway, which Company also had to pay a share of its takings to the Great Eastern. The future plans of this new railway company were already clearly obvious.

I am grateful to Lyn Brooks of the Great Eastern Railway Society for information about the shunting horses at Wivenhoe. Horses do not normally come to mind when discussing railways, and yet in 1911 the Great Eastern Railway owned 1,750. Each was either branded

Sprats for the railway landed at Brightlingsea Hard in the 1920's

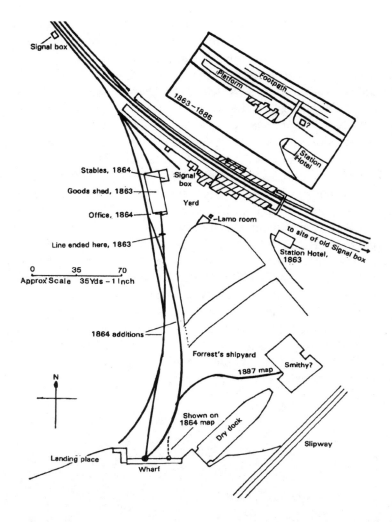

Wivenhoe Station 1897

Signal box

Platform

Footpath

1863 ~ 1886

□?

Station Hotel

Stables, 1864

Signal box

Goods shed, 1863

Yard

Office, 1864

Lamp room

Line ended here, 1863

to site of old Signal box

Station Hotel, 1863

0 35 70
Approx Scale 35 Yds – 1 Inch

1864 additions

Forrest's shipyard

Smithy?

1897 map

N

Shown on
1864 map

Dry dock

Slipway

Landing place

Wharf

on its forefeet with the company's number or wore a small brass plate with the number stamped on it - but whoever heard of a horse referred to as 'Number 1254'?All had pet names given to them by the horse driver or lad who looked after them. By 1900 fodder was being prepared for these horses at a Romford factory on the site of the original locomotive works of the Eastern Counties Railway, the engine works having been moved to Stratford, where they stayed for the rest of the age of steam.

The load these horses pulled was dependent on their weight and limits were laid down in Company Rules about this: for example, a 12-13 cwt horse was used for light parcel wagons, a 14-15 cwt for single goods vans or trolleys, and 15 cwt or over for shunters. One horse, used for shunting at Bishop's Stortford, weighed just over a ton.

When the Great Eastern began to classify its locomotives, horses were always affectionately referred to as 'Class G G'. This Class came to an end when 'Charlie', from the appropriate locality of Newmarket, was let out to grass in 1967. At Wivenhoe the two horses pulled not only railway wagons, but also delivery carts in the town.

The *Station* Hotel, serving horsemen and travellers alike, was opened across the road from the station in 1863. The supplier of beer then, as now, was Cobbolds of Ipswich, John Cobbold, it will be remembered, being a director of the Tendring Hundred Railway. The hotel was at the junction of West Street

and the newly-built Station Road. Also in this road was the Independent Chapel Burial Ground and their School. One wonders how many reprimands were given to early classroom 'train spotters' when the Brightlingsea line was opened; perhaps the Victorian policy of building high windows in schools to stop pupils looking out was justified.

By 1863 the Tendring Hundred Railway had appeared to have accepted the loss of one of its directors and the chance of reaching Brightlingsea and had obtained authorization to construct the 14 miles of line to Walton, starting from the Brightlingsea Railway a quarter of a mile outside Wivenhoe Station, although no start had yet been made by W & B R C.

Things seemed to be going well

Station Road, Wivenhoe, showing the Station Hotel on the right and the high Great Eastern signals. A postcard about 1910

21

though. On 13th February, 1863, a shareholders' meeting had been held, lasting only a few minutes, at which Sir Claude reported that the Line was in a flourishing state with nearly £16,000 of the £25,000 capital already subscribed.

On 23rd December the T H R were unhappy about the delay to their line and sought permission of Parliament to use the line of the W & B R C for the start of their line to Weeley.

By this time, however, the engineers and contractors had been chosen. The Engineer to the Company was James Cooke, who had surveyed the Hythe to Wivenhoe section of the Tendring Hundred Railway in 1858. His assistant was J Olroyd Greaves, a friend of Sir Claude. The Contractor was William Munro, with over 20 years experience of building railways - and not many could better that in the early 1860s! Not only had he built railways in this part of England, but also in the Crimea, France and Ireland. He had recently completed the building of the Colne Valley Line and was a man of considerable reputation. Mr J C Hill was the Contractor's Engineer and Mr Strong the Clerk of Works.

Work began on 21st September, 1863, with the Turning of the First Sod Ceremony, the major event of any Victorian railway.

The Wivenhoe Volunteer Band, under the direction of the local baker, Mr Franks, struck up 'See the Conquering Hero Comes' as the 11.27 steamed into Wivenhoe Station that Monday morning. None of the Lords of the Manor had bothered to leave his home, George Bradley claiming that he had a 'domestic affliction' and the news-papers, when reporting the proceedings, showed their feelings by referring to them as 'The Yorkshire Capitalists'. It all seemed to have a hastily put together look from the start, and gave the sense of someone having said a week before in a strong Yorkshire accent, "Come on, let's get it over with!"

Sir Claude walked down the road from Wivenhoe Hall to meet the Colchester dignitaries from the train and even one of those did not arrive until halfway through the luncheon. Word had, at least, got round Wivenhoe and a large group of locals had gathered to follow the party and see what was happening.

First they walked from the station to Brook Field where the first sod was to be cut: the spot was by Paget Road where a large factory stands today - it must be remembered that the railway then ended at Wivenhoe Station. Mrs Waters, the Rector's wife, performed the actual ceremony. To ensure that she was not seen staggering about with normal heavy railway equipment, Sir Claude produced a miniature steel spade, the handle tied with white satin bows. The sod was cut, three cheers were given, hats were raised and the sod was wheeled a short way in a new navvy's barrow - even this was a special light-weight model for the occasion.

Sir Claude, not wishing to be left out, dug a second sod shortly afterwards. Then, in a short speech, he explained that in his opinion good fortune always smiled on those who put up the capital if a lady cut the first sod and he hoped that it was true on this occasion.

The band started up a lively tune and the party, still followed by the local sightseers, moved off. One can imagine a frail bird-like Mrs Waters, full of embarrassment, and Sir Claude making sure that he was well to the fore in everything that happened. The day's events would be talked over for years to come!

The luncheon that followed was at the *Park* Hotel in Wivenhoe, where the guests arrived after a walk up the High Street. The Hotel was so new that it was still unlicensed and the champagne had to be sent there from the *Three Cups* in Colchester. The chief food was local oysters, of especially good quality that year. Even during luncheon, the speed of it all was apparent. Alderman Cooke, representing Colchester Corporation (the Mayor was 'busy') turned up in the course of the meal having missed the ceremony completely.

With everybody happy after the meal, the speeches resumed. Sir Claude, possibly noticing the obvious absences, said that he always came to such ceremonies as there was certain to be a good luncheon afterwards; as he had only to walk across the road to attend, how-ever, it was hardly surprising that he was there. He remarked how useful the railway system of England would be in time of attack to rush troops to retaliate. The contractors had promised that the line would be finished within six months [by March, 1864] and he would take a keen interest in its progress living, as he did, so close to the intended route.

Mr James Cooke, one of the Engineers, replied that the line could not be built in six months, but certainly by twelve, and the next year's crop of oysters would certainly be carried from the Colne to London. He then, in his enthusiasm, proposed a toast to Sir Claude and received a reprimand for his eagerness when Sir Claude reminded him that there was a lady present, Mrs Waters, and she deserved priority. Mr Cooke apologised, blamed it on his being a bachelor, and the proceedings settled down again.

William Munro spoke of how the road to Brightlingsea had always been busy and how this railway would open up the town even more. Had the Great Eastern put down all the capital they would have got their money back within the next five years. So, as with the Tendring Hundred Railway, the Great Eastern was there at the beginning.

Now the smoke of a steam locomotive could be seen moving back-wards and forwards between Wivenhoe and Alresford Creek. It was Munro's own locomotive *Cam*, which, along with his other locomotive, *Colne*, was to help build the line. Both purchased in 1863, they were first used for the Colne Valley Railway extension to Haverhill, where *Cam* was damaged in a shed fire.

After the Brightlingsea branch was completed, they were off to Ireland, working in County Clare on the building of the Ennis to Gort section of the Athenny and Ennis Line, which opened in 1869. Their eventual fate is unknown.

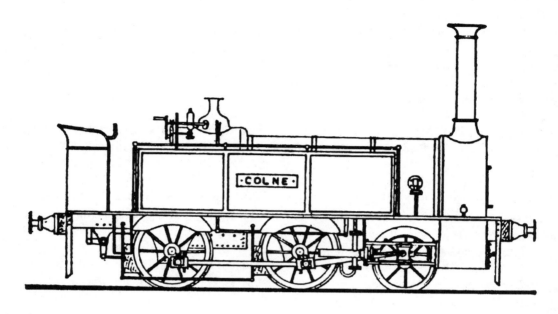

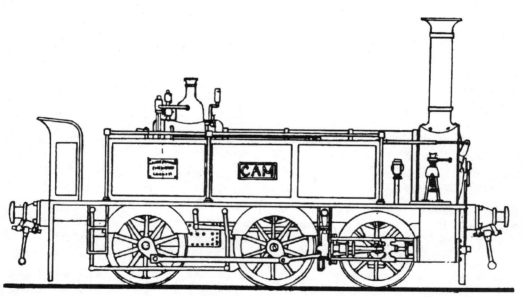

The builders of the line. The contractor's locomotives *Cam* and *Colne* re-united after 130 years.

From then on, it is not easy to trace the outcome of the shareholders' meetings, as the Directors rarely left Yorkshire and meetings were held at Pontefract, close to George Bradley's offices. The date and place was always well advertised in the local paper during the months of February or March, but, as the meetings were rarely reported, any interested shareholder had a long and expensive journey ahead of him if he wished to find out what was happening to his money.

However, the first meeting after the Turning of the First Sod Ceremony was held in London, in Chancery Lane, where a very optimistic mood prevailed. The next was still close to home, in the Guildhall Coffee House, London, on 29th February, 1864. The Engineers were to report that 21 miles of sea wall had been built and had effectively resisted the force of the water during the winter, which had frequently produced very high tides and strong winds. If only Mr Cooke and Mr Greaves had been able to foresee the future of their railway, they would have checked those defences again and again.

The line was, by then, built from Wivenhoe to Alresford Creek and work had been started on the swing bridge spanning the Creek. Upwards of 100 tons of iron lay on the ground ready for the fixing together by men working for Shaws of Birmingham who had gained the contract. Another small mystery here:

What was to come. Flooding of the line, this time the great flood of 1953 (*Photo F Armes*)

why Shaws? Edward Westwood, the man who had put up the money came from Oldswinford, only 15 miles from Birmingham and perhaps he had influenced the award of the work to a firm that he knew well.

The line was to change the lives of many people, for example, Samuel Welham, the occupier of Copyhold Farm on a lonely part of the Wivenhoe marshland near Alresford Creek. Within two years he was to have a railway running past, only yards from his front door. Eight years later the property had been re-named White House. Had Samuel been unable to continue as a farmer following the railway's intrusion?

George Bradley cheered the Guildhall meeting by stating that the final cost of construction would be less than £40,000 and already railways were paying big dividends. At Lynn in Norfolk they were paying out 6% on an outlay of £80,000. In addition to sprat traffic it was also suggested that if yachtsmen could lay up their craft at Brightlingsea instead of Portsmouth or Cowes (and why not, for London was only a short distance away), it would mean passengers for the railway and, as each yacht had a crew of six or so, more trade for the town.

About then things started to go wrong for the Contractor, William Munro. It seems that he was trying to do too many things at once. It soon became apparent that the line would not be ready by September, 1864, and the once-suggested date of the previous March was ridiculous. As September came and went the Tendring Hundred Directors became more and more irritable. They wanted the use of the line from Wivenhoe Station to the Brightlingsea Line junction in order to carry out their proposed extension to Weeley. Although the Contractor's locomotive ran happily along this section, it certainly was not yet ready for passenger traffic - it would seem that Munro's statement to the Company Meeting that the line was all ready was an exaggeration.

An ultimatum was given: the W & B R C had until 1st November to complete this section otherwise the T H R C would do so and send the bill.

In October, Munro was given £1,000 by the Directors in return for a promise that the line would be ready by the next January. A ballast field at Moveron's Farm, Brightlingsea, then known as Mr Mason's farm, as it had been leased to him by Nicolas Magens, was given over for the building of the line from the swing bridge to Brightlingsea Station.

Of course, Munro failed to meet the November deadline and the T H R C Directors went ahead as threatened at the Wivenhoe and Brightlingsea Company's expense. They were no doubt delighted at getting their own back on the company that had stolen their hoped-for line and also their Chairman. Liability for payment and the amount due were the subject of dispute for 11 years, when the W & B paid £7,000 to the T H R.

Things went from bad to worse for Munro and were to come to an unhappy end the following year during the building of the proposed Mistley, Thorpe and Walton Railway, a line that never

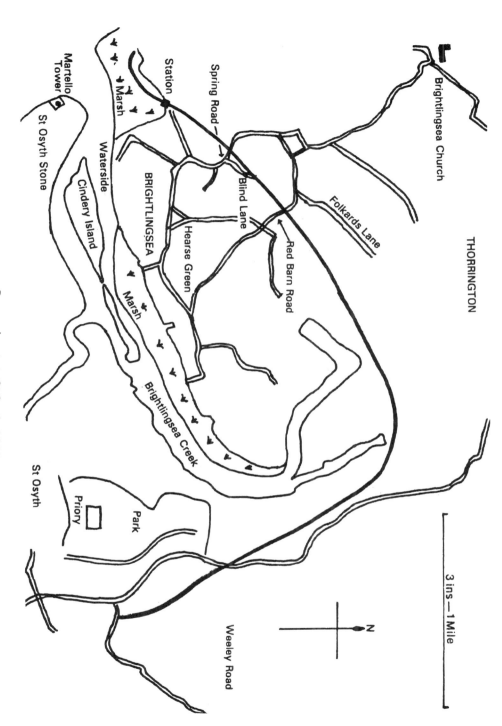

Proposed route to St Osyth, 1864

27

came into being. Progress on that line was slow, but Munro refused to give up possession of the works. In April, 1865, a pitched battle took place between a band of Munro's navvies and sixty longshoremen recruited from Harwich led by the Company's Engineer. Munro's Agent, Mr Fryer, placed himself at the head of a cutting and refused to move. A hard-fought battle ensued and finally Fryer and his men were beaten back. This still did not settle the affair and Fryer had to be personally ejected from the site three times before construction could continue.

It might have been this incident that made the Directors fear for the future of the line, for it was about then that the scheme was abandoned, the earth works being visible to this day. Munro became bankrupt after this and similar failures, although letters of support and condemnation were to rage in the *Essex Standard* for quite a while afterwards.

Work on the Brightlingsea Line was delayed while Peter Bruff, the Tendring Hundred Engineer, was hired to take over its construction. All this knocked the completion date off course and the sale of shares suffered. The Great Eastern Railway saw its chance and stepped in, offering to buy a third of the shares to enable the work to continue. It was giving itself a very good bargaining position for the future which must have been fully realised at the time. It had 70% of the Tendring shares and what was to become 40% of the Wivenhoe and Brightlingsea Railway.

A proposal was put forward in November, 1864, to extend the line beyond Brightlingsea Railway Station, when completed, to St Osyth, a village that had been completely ignored in the railway plans for north-east Essex. This was a difficult proposition. Even today Brightlingsea is a 'one road in, one road out of' town, as the surrounding marshland is too costly to build roads on and a bridge across the Brightlingsea Creek, while certainly being spectacular, is not, and never has been, financially viable.

The Great Eastern, whose suggestion it was, planned to take a marshland route in the shape of an inverted U. The line would lead out of Brightlingsea going through the town, turn at the head of Flag Creek, run parallel to the St Osyth Road, then turn past the Priory and into St Osyth village, then known as Chich St Osyth, 'chich' meaning creek. Most of the Thorrington land was owned by Felix Francis and St John's College, Cambridge. All these plans, as was quite usual, came to nothing and, when finished, the railway terminated at Brightlingsea.

The St Osyth idea, however, stayed in the minds of the railway planners for years afterwards. In 1872, the Tendring Hundred and Great Eastern planned a railway from west of Weeley Station on the Walton Line, to St Osyth and then on to Clacton, plans even getting approved by Parliament in November. Clacton itself had even tried to be reached by the Tendring Hundred idea of a line from Thorpe in 1864: eventually in 1882 the Great Eastern built a line from Thorpe to Clacton.

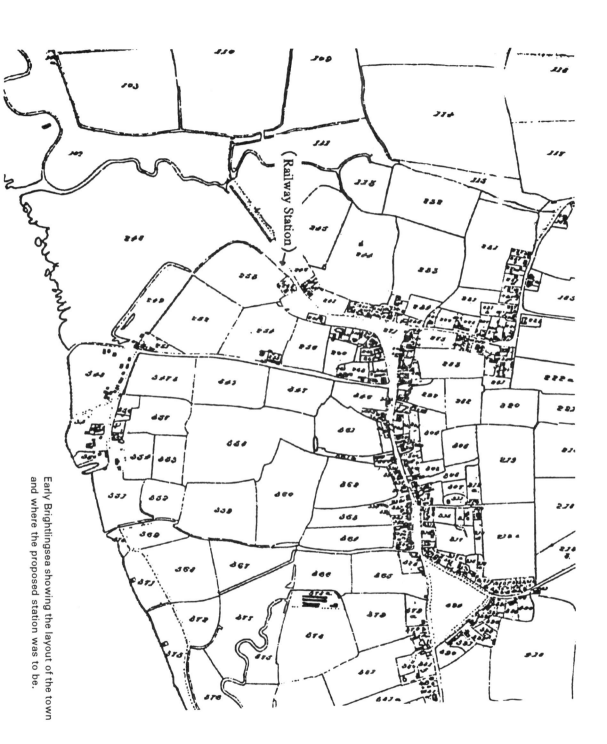

Early Brightlingsea showing the layout of the town and where the proposed station was to be.

With the swing bridge completed in 1865, the Brightlingsea Railway pushed forward to its terminus. The town of Brightlingsea can best be thought of as a letter Y lying on its left side. The stem of the Y ended at Hurst (then spelt Hearse) Green: the upper stroke ended at Spring Corner, while the lower at a small row of cottages close to where the new railway station was to be situated. Some of the owners of these cottages recall old Brightlingsea families and have a Victorian sound to them - Ebenezer Root, Sarah Jolly, Benjamin Went and William Root.

The station area itself consisted of Marshland, cut in two by a sea wall. On one side was West Marsh Saltings - common land which ended at the sea: and on the landward side was Weller's Marsh, owned by William Root .

This area had been a popular one with the Brightlingsea locals. During summer evenings the sea wall was a well-used walking place, especially for courting couples, sometimes 150 people could be seen on a warm evening. The Wall led to a ford across Alresford Creek dating from Roman times, there having been a Roman villa at nearby Noah's Ark. The Wall, being far shorter than the journey by road, would certainly have been used by travellers to Wivenhoe or Alresford who had little luggage to carry.

Access to Weller's Marsh could be gained by a gate, but most of the pastimes, including the courting, took place on the wild marsh itself. In the summer it was a favourite swimming spot for local boys and, when the weather was

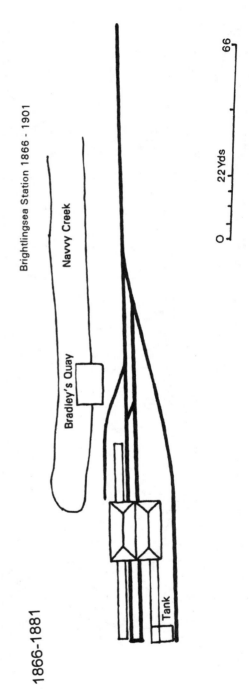

Brightlingsea Station 1866 - 1901

Navvy Creek

Bradley's Quay

Tank

1866-1881

66

22 Yds

0

30

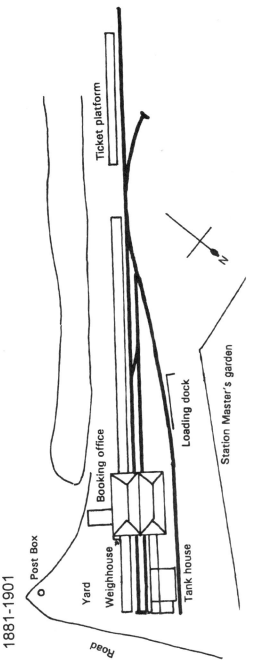

1881-1901

Post Box

Yard

Weighhouse

Booking office

Ticket platform

Loading dock

Tank house

Station Master's garden

Road

N

not so kind, there were always crabs to be caught in the many small creeks - one area was shortly to become known as The Crabwell for that reason. Sportsmen too, some legal, some not, would shoot at anything edible. On the land where the Station was to stand, people would gather for games. Cricket, bat and ball games and quoits were the favourites.

The advent of the railway put a stop to the marshland walks, as the line had to be crossed and to trespass on the rail-way was to invite prosecution and reports of cases of this frequently appeared in local newspapers.

The station was about 20 feet high and in the shape of a double barn, with a sloping roof, rather like an inverted W when seen from an approaching train, the centre being supported on metal poles. It was built of wood with roofing felt over the top section. After a few years' weathering it had the appearance of being slate-grey in colour, possibly from neglect after its initial coat of creosote. The train entered on the right of two sets of rails and pulled up alongside a three feet high platform. The left-hand side was kept for special occasions recalls Chris Jolly, an old engine driver, thinking back over 80 years.

It was as well that the line was opened in the spring, leaving the effect of the strong on-shore winter wind blowing straight through those buildings to be discovered at a later date.

A tank house was built to provide thirsty engines with water - and that was all, at least as far as the Railway was concerned. There was an area to the rear

of these buildings for the Stationmaster to use as a garden. It was a simple station for those days, although at that time the main Colchester Station had the look of a wooden-planked cow barn.

A natural harbour for the intended sprat boats was found at the head of Navvy Creek, a small inlet running towards the Station, where a landing stage - to be called Bradley's Quay in honour of George Bradley - was planned. It consisted of 12 upright pillars about 12 to 14 feet long surmounted by a platform of thick timbers with sunk bolts. The whole structure measured 20 x 10 feet: it was to be served by a short branch line running from the main track.

The town seemed the perfect answer to the sprat problem. The fish could be landed at any time - or so they thought - and Brightlingsea Creek itself was

navigable by sprat boats even at low tide. Talk began to grow among the Directors as to how Brightlingsea would develop. Grimsby and Lowestoft had grown from small fishing villages to huge fishing ports - and these had no sheltered harbours. The harbour facilities at Brightlingsea were there and, with its easy access to London, it could develop in an even bigger way. The sprats need no longer lie in gleaming heaps on local fields in winter months, rotting to provide manure for next year's crops and feeding the seabirds, but could be sold at a far greater profit. Three hundred vessels a year came into Brightlingsea and many thousands of tons of sprats were being wasted.

It would mean quite a change in the everyday life of the town too. The solitary road in and out of the town had meant isolation. One might court a girl from Thorrington at the end of that road, but more often than not you married a local girl.

In 1832 letters arrived in the town by foot post from Thorpe at 4 p.m. and letters were carried by foot post to Colchester at 5 p.m. The railway was going to link Brightlingsea far more with the outside world.

In 1835 there were three carriers to Colchester taking it in turns to go each

day, but in 1848 a cart and a van carried daily to Colchester and a horse-drawn omnibus covered the distance on Mondays, Wednesdays and Saturdays.

As if in preparation for the coming of the railway, the town had kept up with modern inventions, becoming gas lit in 1862.

The arrival of the railway led to an interesting prosecution: a hut on West Marsh was used as an inn to give the navvies working on the line beer and thus stop them wasting time going into the town for refreshments; it probably stopped a good few fights as well and so served a very useful purpose. P.C. Trubshoe, the town's first and, then, only constable, possibly thought so too, but he had his job to do. The inn had no signboard as required by law and its owner was prosecuted and fined 50 shillings, with 10 shillings and sixpence costs. Maybe Trubshoe had been involved in some incident with the navvies that had left him with a grudge, for, as no signboard appeared, the owner was taken to court again. The magistrates had the charge withdrawn on payment of costs and from then on the matter was allowed to rest.

P. C. Charles Christmas Trubshoe, Brightlingsea's first policeman and prosecutor of the railway.

CAT AND MOUSE GAME

On the morning of 17th April, 1866, little work could have been done in Brightlingsea and, before long, the afternoon crowds must have filled the station area waiting for the first white puffs of smoke to be seen across the marshland. Due to a ninety degree curve in the last half mile of track before the station a train could easily be seen for some five minutes before its arrival; a great boon to the impatient or those awaiting loved ones.

On this day a special train had left London at 11 a.m. to carry the Directors to Brightlingsea, for the Line was at last going to be opened. All the Yorkshire Directors had travelled down and were to be met by Sir Claude de Crespigny at Wivenhoe Station before starting off for Brightlingsea in the afternoon sunshine. A halt was made to inspect the 'Iron Viaduct' over Alresford Creek - 'One of the most important structures of its kind in this part of the Kingdom', commented the local press.

The train steamed into Brightlingsea Station to be greeted by William Abbot (the Stationmaster) and local dignitaries. A rather late oyster luncheon was held in the goods area of the Station, after which the guests strolled proudly round the town, noting various improvements in both building and trade and speculating on just how much more the railway could do to improve the town and boost their shares.

The Swing Bridge over Alresford Creek.

The Swing Bridge opens on to its support piers.

Despite the late luncheon, their tour of the town over, back they went to Colchester, where a 'sumptuous dinner' was awaiting them in the *Cups* Hotel at 5 p.m. The sunshine continued on the journey back, one reporter noting that 'With brilliant sunshine and high tide, the trip was a most enjoyable one'.

The Dinner over, the speeches began and lengthy and patronising they were too! One of the first was to 'The Army, Navy and Volunteers' - Colonel Sir Claude had brought his friends with him: it was acknowledged by Colonel Palmer, Captain Brant and Colonel Mosley.

Mr Waddy commented that, from what he had seen that day, he looked upon Brightlingsea as a very important place and, indeed, he had been indulging in a sort of daydream in which he saw the Brightlingsea of the future overshadow the Brighton of the day.

Mr C H Tanner for the Directors of the Great Eastern Railway Company made his first move in what was to be a cat and mouse game lasting almost 25 years. He was quick to state that he 'supposed the first and foremost reason that he and his colleagues wished the line every success was because the G.E.R. had contributed such a large proportion of the Capital'. At a celebration where backslapping was very much in order and the *Standard* report is punctuated with comments such as 'mild applause' and 'laughter' an out-of-place silence greeted this remark. As Mr Tanner continued his speech, the non-G.E.R. directors must have reflected that his company had supplied one third of the capital - £8,500 - and was to collect 40% of the receipts. There was also a clause in the Wivenhoe & Brightlingsea Act to say that, if ever it was considered necessary, they could sell out to the Great Eastern. All very dangerous!

Mr George Smith, another G.E.R. director, was the next to speak and he too made the tongue in cheek comment of complimenting James Robinson on having come such a long way to give his services to the Company and reminding him that he could see that he was 'small in stature, but extremely large in heart'.

Then came a reference to that other rival, the Tendring Hundred Railway, and possibly its help in its construction, for Smith continued that he hoped the friction would now end and that, in future, they could work together. "Just think how the Brightlingsea line would benefit the Wivenhoe and Colchester traffic, and therefore the T H R." A beautiful job of smoothing things over by a director of a company that was working both lines for a fair share of the profits.

Speechmaking over, the directors began their return to Yorkshire or Warwickshire, Sir Claude to army life, and the people of Brightlingsea to their normal daily lives - that were never to be quite the same again.

The Swing Bridge over Alresford Creek and the manning of it was to

The T bar that opened the bridge. The gear wheel, some 12ft across, had 'ball bearings the size of footballs'.

determine the progress and the eventual closure of the line. It was 430 feet long on large concrete pillars. The centre span swung open through 90° and rested, when open, on two wooden piled piers rising from the riverbed. It was built in this way to allow shipping to pass, as, at high tide, the only time that the Creek is navigable, there was insufficient clearance of a fixed bridge.

When the Bridge was used after the opening of the Line it allowed ships to pass through to Thorrington Tide Mill. This mill, of which there are only 3 or 4 similar in England, still stands and was used for grinding flour. The term 'Tide Mill' relates to the twin gates which were opened for the incoming tide to allow a pond behind the mill to fill: at full tide the gates were closed, trapping the water as the tide went down. The trapped water was used to turn a water wheel powering the three grindstones of the mill. A cheap source of power, replenished twice a day.

In latter days the Bridge was opened to allow the ships to reach the Alresford Sand & Ballast Company's pier on the north side of the Creek, just above the Bridge. It was served by an aerial bucket lift, the remains of which could still be seen in 1984.

The Bridge was usually left open for shipping two hours before and after high tide, and only closed if a train was due. Originally, two men from Alresford would row out to the centre of the Bridge to open or close it. This was done by means of a 'T' bar inserted in a cog in the centre span. This would be turned, rotating a large ball race, with ball

bearings reported to be 'as big as footballs'. The gear itself is estimated to have been some 12 feet in diameter with the teeth 4 inches deep and 3 inches across.

The reason for the two-man operation can be seen from the following explanation - one man could walk across the Bridge and open the centre span until it rested on the support piers: there he would remain until after the passing of the boat, closing the span when it had passed. While the Bridge was open the second man would row out to a support

The Bridge, with the Pilotman's cottage in the background, and the red flag warning shipping of the bridge.

pier in case the mechanism failed and the centre span remained open, marooning the number one who would be unable to get off the centre span or go anywhere for help. The stations were much too far away for any pitiful cries for help to be heard. In the case of it remaining open for a longer period of time, as at the high tide - a practice discontinued in later times - the man would be taken off by boat and returned later.

As an act of good faith the man operating the bridge (known as the Bridge Pilot) would ride across in the cab of the train, not just after the Bridge had been closed, but on every train, getting off at the further side. This was not only to control the speed of the train, but was one way of ensuring that he had done his work properly!

The boat was also used for oiling the mechanical parts, a job constantly needing to be done in the salt spray and high winds that frequently hit the Bridge.

Distortion of the rails in summer heat could cause danger and was yet another reason why the Bridge Pilot rode across in the train. When the gap between the rails in the centre did close, the simple and ingenious operation was for the Pilot to tip out a short piece of rail in the centre of the Bridge and replace them with rails of shorter length.

A speed restriction of 10, later 5, miles per hour was put on the Bridge: a speed not always easy to judge in engines with no speedometers and which, were the brakes not released soon enough, would easily come to a halt. The Brightlingsea people were to take an instant dislike to the Bridge, which was to last the life of the Line. It swayed considerably, they said, especially in high winds - and quite a bit at other times too! It was frequently checked, as regulations demanded, but there can still be little doubt that quite a lot of traffic was lost after the coming of the 'bus service due to these unfounded fears.

Bridge procedure for the locomotive drivers was strictly observed. On approaching the Bridge and passing the. short semaphore signals permanently set at 'Caution', three clear blasts of the whistle were given and the train was brought to a halt beside the Bridge stop signal post for the Pilot to climb aboard and ride over the Bridge.

At dusk it was the Pilot's job to light the lamps at the Bridge Stop and Distant Signals at each end of the Bridge. These would be kept burning all night and were also needed in foggy weather - estimated by the ability to see a fixed signal at 200 yards. The same 'test' was used during falling snow. When the Bridge was closed to river traffic a red flag by day or a red light for the dark were fixed to the centre of the Bridge. The red flag in the centre of the bridge was used as a test of a driver's railway knowledge. The question would be asked, "Where is the only place a driver may drive his locomotive past a red flag?" Of course, the flag was there to warn the shipping, not the railwaymen. The night signal also needed lighting, so the work of the Bridge Pilot was a busy and demanding one, entailing many varied tasks.

Just towards the turn of the century a

cottage was built for the Bridge Pilot, some 200 yards on the Wivenhoe side of the Bridge on the landward side of the railway, while a rowing boat, owned by the railway, was kept in a small hut, eventually made of corrugated iron, on the north side of the Bridge. A footpath ran from the cottage along the side of the Creek towards Alresford and is still there today, as are the boatshed and the remains of the cottage garden.

The Bridge was to be given many titles: Iron Bridge in early documents, Swing Bridge in later years and Ford Bridge to the people of Brightlingsea. I shall continue to use the name 'Swing Bridge' or confusion may occur in the following pages!

The notice that was nailed to the door of Brightlingsea Station mentioned little of the W & B R C; in fact, the heading of Great Eastern Railway was almost as large as the rest of the information. It was as sure that their name would be there as it was that their locomotives hauled the trains.

Sadly, nothing is known of the first locomotive that pulled the Directors' train or those of many years afterwards, the reason being that when Robert Sinclaire became Superintendent of the new Great Eastern Railway in 1862, the

GREAT EASTERN RAILWAY.

OPENING
WIVENHOE & BRIGHTLINGSEA RAILWAY.

The Line from **WIVENHOE** to **BRIGHTLINGSEA** will be Opened for Traffic on Wednesday, 18th April, 1866, and Trains will be run as under:—

BY ORDER.

39

company was an amalgamation of several eastern lines, the largest being the Eastern Counties Railway. Each of these lines had its own locomotives and Sinclaire inherited some one hundred of all shapes and sizes and was, eventually, to bring an air of order to what had been an infinite variety. It could have been any of these locomotives that worked the Line at first and it is doubtful if its identity will ever be known. Its colour can, at least, be guessed at, for during Sinclaire's stay with the G E R the engines were usually light green with chocolate coloured frames.

The rolling stock would have consisted of four wheel carriages once belonging to the Eastern Counties Railway. The only means of braking the stock would have been a hand operated brake in the Guard's Van. If there were any lights in the carriages, which is doubtful, they would have been oil lamps and there is no exaggeration whatsoever in supposing that any person wishing to read at night on the 15 minute journey from Wivenhoe to Brightlingsea that left Wivenhoe at 8.15 p.m. on a weekday would have to carry a candle lantern to do so, although for so short a journey it might hardly have been worthwhile. With no heating either, it must have been a depressing ride on a rainy winter's night.

For the driver and fireman the trip would be a typical example of the hardship endured by Victorian workmen. In the open cab that was common in early locos, while their fronts were being overheated by the fire, their backs would be almost numb with cold and their faces, far removed from the heat, would be half frozen. One only has to walk across the Brightlingsea Marsh on a winter's day with a northerly wind blowing to get some impression of these conditions and, added to it, the locomotive would be travelling at 30 miles per hour or more. The obvious answer would be to get down close to the fire, but a look-out had to be kept. The small porthole windows were, if not coated with grime from the engine, often unreliable, so the crew had to put their faces round the side of the cab into the wind to keep a watch, through tears, for the signals ahead.

The suggestion has been made that the reason engine drivers are often shown in old photographs wearing beards is quite simple - the whiskers could be wrapped around the face on winter's nights such as those!

Sometimes the look-out windows were too high for the drivers, who would carry around their own wooden box to stand on if it was necessary to use the windows!

The locomotive had, however, at least one advantage - for providing hot food for the engine crew. Breakfast for these men was often a bloater or kipper cooked over the locomotive fire on a carefully cleaned shovel .

One would have expected a better service on the new line than four trains each way on weekdays, but that's all there were and even one of those was a goods train with 'coaches attached for the convenience of passengers'. Travellers were advised to get to the station five minutes early in order to be 'booked in'. The trains went via Colchester, St Botolph's, before arriving at Colchester Main Station, often called 'The North' by the people of the area. This was to be the established route for the life of the Line.

St Botolph's, opened only a month before, was designed primarily to serve the new Military Barracks then under construction, but it was later to prove of great convenience to shoppers. Possibly Sir Claude de Crespigny, who had connections with both the Wivenhoe and Brightlingsea and, formerly, the Tendring Hundred Railways, had a say in the idea of assisting his army colleagues. The Tendring Hundred were to use St Botolph's for their Board Meetings from then onwards.

The Third Class fare to Colchester from Brightlingsea was 1s.2d [6p.], but, if one was prepared to suffer a journey sitting on bare wooden boards, there was always the Parliamentary Class at 9½d. [4p.].

The Parliamentary train fares of one penny a mile, although seemingly cheap, did not fulfil the Duke of Wellington's fears when railways were first introduced, that they would 'encourage the masses to move about'. A bare board journey to London by Parliamentary fare would cost 5s. [25p.], taking 4 hours, 10 minutes, while the expresses took 2½

Bradley's Quay in the late 1920s. The unsuccessful idea for the off loading of sprats. (*Len Lewes collection*)

The remains of Bradley's Quay at Brightlingsea after the
concrete sea wall had been built in 1925 (*Len Lewes collection*)

hours. Added to this, how many people
in that day who would be likely to use
the Parliamentary Trains would want to
go to London any way? The
Brightlingsea 'world' ended at Colchester
and the simple Third Class fare was
probably as much as they wished to pay.

Brightlingsea was never to become,
as Mr Waddy had hoped, 'the Brighton
of the future'. Bradley's Quay could not
possibly work effectively, as there was
not enough water, even at high tides, for
large vessels. It was eventually to help
the shrimp boats, which would pass the
Quay, situated at the end of Navvy
Creek, at high tide, mooring up at the
Station to unload. The depth of the Creek
at full tide was only 8 feet and, as the
shrimpers needed only 5 feet of water, an
easily accessible dock was found close to
the railway.

Shortly after the opening of the Line,
George Bradley's time as a speculator
was coming to an end. He had become
personally involved in the building of the
Quay, using £6,000 of his own money,
always believing that it could be dredged
or used for other purposes, now he had
no money left to help his plans further
forward.

A locked gate was eventually to
separate the siding from the running line,
as the shrimpers could quite easily handle
their baskets on to the station platform
themselves. The top platform of the Quay
was never fully completed and the
upright pillars were left sticking up out of
the mud until the West Marsh
development of the 1930s. It became a
good play area for local children who
liked running along its top and jumping
off into the Crabwell Fleets, as the

Navvy Creek entrance became called.

The sidings of the Quay were taken up as well. Mr Wheeler, who came to the line as a young porter in 1919 recalls sleeper marks branching off the main track and seeming to run nowhere.

Within a year of the opening of the Railway, Sir Claude de Crespigny was dead. This true Victorian speculator and man of humour contracted cancer of the tongue and died painfully a few months later.

His eldest son, also called Claude, inherited his father's title, but in a very short while had resigned his Army Commission, possibly only accepted to please father, and was to become a notable local eccentric, fighting would-be servants to prove their worth and pestering Blondin to let him go on the tightrope with him. His full, very amusing story can be read in *Essex Eccentrics* by Alison Barnes.

Richard Moxon now became Chairman, so the ownership of the Railway remained firmly north-country based.

The Railway was now to enter a period of prosperity. The sprat venture may have failed, but Brightlingsea developed as a principal breeding and packing town for oysters, and the age of the steam yacht had arrived.

The original service of four trains each way per day (one carrying mixed freight) was maintained for some years, but, as Brightlingsea expanded and trade increased, more trains were added.

By the 1890s there were eight trains each way a day and two or three were added to Sunday services to cope with the summer excursions.

It is not to be thought that Brightlingsea was the only expanding town. With the push of the railway towards Walton, Wivenhoe was to gain three hotels built within a few years of each other. The *Station* Hotel has ready been mentioned, but the *Grosvenor* and the *Park* hotels were also built for the new visitors, many of these arriving as Wivenhoe gained importance in the yachting world.

In August, 1876, the Company, following a quarrel with the Great Eastern, ordered its own locomotive from Hudswell Clarke of Leeds. They had decided to try and exist independent of the Great Eastern who had been providing the rolling stock. It was a small outside cylinder 0-6-0 Tank Engine, with 3 ft 3 in wheels and a total weight of 26 tons. The maker's order number was 184, but on arrival at the Line it was promptly named *Resolute* and given the number 'One'. It seems that the company might have intended to buy more. Two new carriages were also bought to use with the new locomotive.

The manufacturer's original colour for *Resolute* was maroon and it seems that this colour was retained. Chris Jolly, when one hundred years old, recalled, "I did hear tell of a red engine which ran on the Line and was there before I was... but it was not red, more a sort of reddish brown."

The Great Eastern was naturally unhappy about all this and, at a Shareholders' Meeting the following year, expressed a wish to take over the Line

RESOLUTE No. 1 - G.E.R. 203

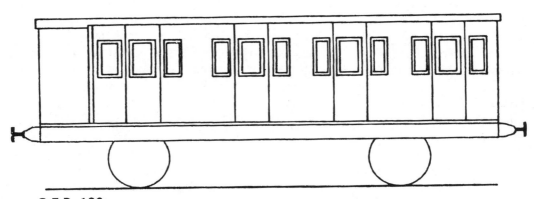

G.E.R. 126

G.E.R. 125   *Resolute*, the line's only personal locomotive with her two carriages. It was to run the line for only two years. 1877 -1879

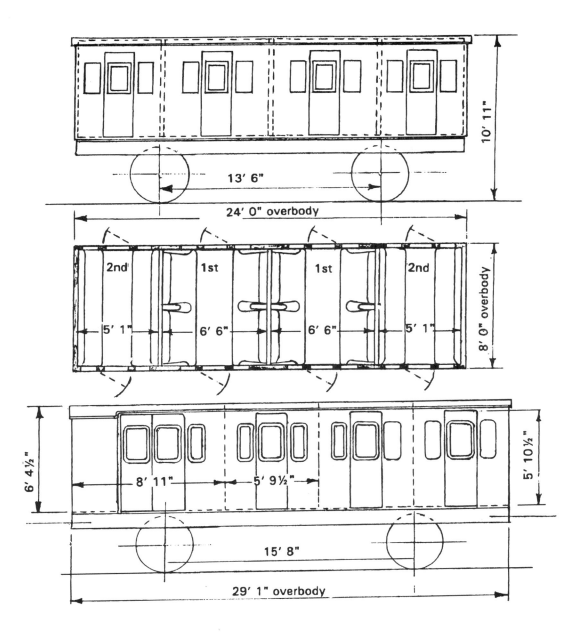

Resolute's two carriages.

again.

This bid for independence could have been the sound beginnings for an independent W & B R C, but things started to go wrong. George Bradley, already having lost on the concept of a sprat quay, suffered other setbacks. In 1874 a depression in the coal industry, in which he had many investments, left him constantly short of money and many of his speculations had to be mortgaged. In 1889 he was forced to sell his colliery hares to pay off his debts and the following year his estate, Ackton Hall, was up for sale, while he moved into the far less grand Rectory House. So influential had he grown that the bulk of his estate was sold for £192,000.

He was finally to become bankrupt in 1897 and, as proof of the extent of his speculations, the trustees had to take away five tons of paperwork from his offices. He was dead 8 years later.

His name was perpetuated in a public house, a street and a quay. The *Bradley Arms* and Bradley Street are in Castleford, and Bradley's Quay was to remain with the Brightlingsea scene until the 1930s. Although the name may be remembered, sadly no known portrait of him exists.

The Lords of the Manor had, in fact, started selling out in 1871. The title was even given to the wife of Edward Westwood for one year in 1886, when Elizabeth Pill-Westwood became Lord of the Manor of Brightlingsea. One suspects that this was more for the novel experience than for anything else!

Due perhaps to all this disruption or possibly because *Resolute* proved inadequate for its job, the Great Eastern resumed working the line again on 1st September, 1879, three years after the attempted break away. Proud *Resolute* was now no longer 'No.1', but 203 of the Great Eastern Railway. It was only suitable for light work and was withdrawn in March, 1888, having been condemned the year before and, after being kept in Stratford Works Machine Shop (Stratford being the Headquarters of the Great Eastern), was broken up in July, 1890.

The two carriages were also taken over; one was a First Class fitted with a brake and numbered 126 by the Great Eastern; no picture remains of the other which was a mixed class (composite) 29 ft 6 ins long, suggesting it was not of Great Eastern origin. They were withdrawn in 1898, by which time they had been considerably modernised, being fitted with gas lighting in 1896 and with Westinghouse brakes by 1890.

Another coach, also a composite, G.E.R. number 125 was used on the line in the late 1870s. It had been inherited by the G.E.R. in 1879 in a batch of five from the Thetford and Watton Railway and was another 'non-conformist' type in the Great Eastern's varied stock. What eventually happened to it and the interesting part would play in the line's history will appear later.

Although things seemed to be going badly for both the Company and George Bradley, it seems that others fared worse.

The *Station* Hotel tenant, Mr G S Cook, received a letter from Cobbold's

Brewery at the end of August, 1878, reading - 'Sir, we are persuaded that you are doing no good for yourself and us, and you ought to take the earliest opportunity to give up the *Station* Hotel. We have given you a good opportunity to recover yourself this Summer, and all the while you have been going backwards instead of forwards.' Enclosed with the letter was a simple form for the recipient to sign agreeing to give up possession one month later.

Problems occurred too at Brightlingsea Station. Although the carrier's cart was still running and was to continue to do so until the 1930s, the carriers themselves tending to remain in business for a long while, the Station Masters changed frequently: Abbot in 1866, Dale in 1870, Howlett in 1878, Howard in 1882 and Sergeant in 1888, but during this time Mr Fuller remained constant as the Parcels Agent. Perhaps the life of a Station Master had its difficulties.

With the ever-expanding Great Eastern once again in control, more alterations were made. Firstly, in 1881, the double barn that was Brightlingsea Railway Station. An interesting addition was the Ticket Platform, in advance of the actual Station Platform, where trains would be halted for ticket collection before proceeding to the Station, where the passengers would join in a 'free for all' for the exit. Perhaps the idea of a trampled ticket collector was not quite in keeping with Victorian decorum.

The Station itself became a more imposing structure with the addition of a Booking Office, coal shed and weigh

Ted Hills, the regular guard on the Brightlingsea train, in Great Eastern uniform.

house. The hopes for Bradley's Quay were finally abandoned and all traces of it were removed from the map of the new Station layout.

On Easter Monday, 1882, the new additions to the station were to witness quite a disturbance. Many people came for the day on the morning train, but, shortly after its arrival, a fight broke out between Brightlingsea and Colchester youths on the land adjoining the Creek, the local recreation area. Sticks, stones or any other weapons that could be found were used and the fight became so fierce that Chief Officer Smith of the Coastguard had to call out his men. They arrived armed to sort it all out, which

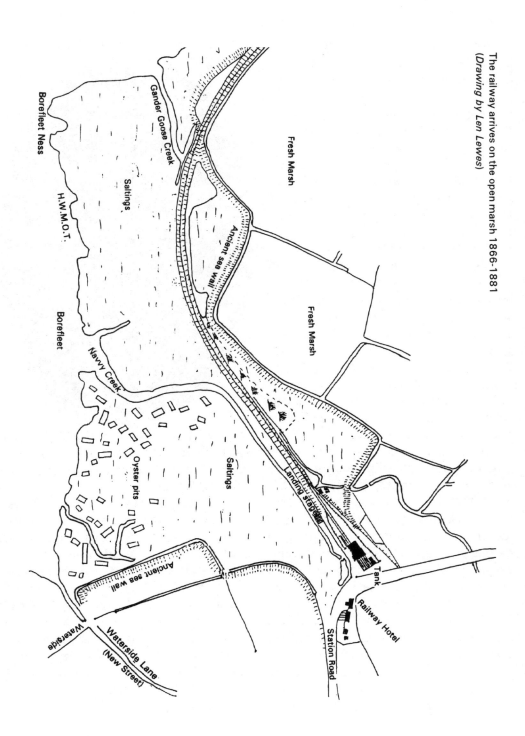

The railway arrives on the open marsh 1866-1881
(*Drawing by Len Lewes*)

Borefleet Ness

Gander Goose Creek

Saltings

H.W.M.O.T.

Borefleet

Navvy Creek

Oyster pits

Saltings

Ancient sea wall

Waterside

Waterside Lane
(New Street)

Fresh Marsh

Ancient sea wall

Fresh Marsh

Landing stage

Tank

Railway Hotel

Station Road

48

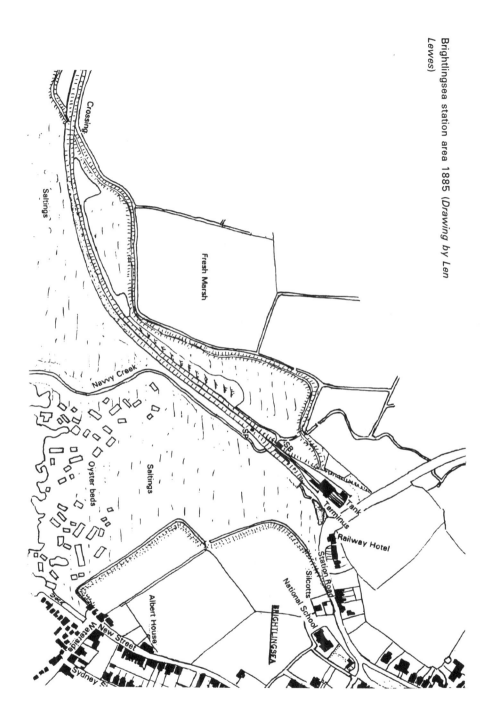

Brightlingsea station area 1885 (*Drawing by Len Lewes*)

Crossing

Saltings

Fresh Marsh

Navvy Creek

Saltings

Oyster beds

SB

SB

Tank

Terminus

Railway Hotel

Station Road

Silcotts

National School

BRIGHTLINGSEA

Albert House

New Street

Waterside

Sydney

they did after a difficult time. In the evening, when the Colchester lads came to catch their last train home, the Brightlingsea boys were waiting for them and it was not until the train left at 7.08 p.m that things quietened down.

The Coastguard Station, at the bottom of Sydney Street, was founded to combat the smuggling for which Brightlingsea and Wivenhoe seemed well situated. Coastguards' jobs included protection against invasion from the sea, assisting in times of ship-wreck, transporting passengers to and from St Osyth Stone when ferrymen had gone home and patrolling the coast from St Osyth Stone towards Clacton, where they met Clacton Coastguard Officers about halfway to exchange a password as proof of meeting.

In 1886 Wivenhoe Station too was rebuilt and looked, at least on the side that has not been demolished, similar to its present state. The Victorian press estimated its cost at £5,000, the down platform being 450 feet long and the up 500 feet. The contractor was O T Gibbons of Ipswich. Searching for something to say, the newspaper told its readers that 400,000 bricks were to be used in its construction and also reported a gruesome item that, as the bridge girders were being unloaded, a workman had two fingers crushed "the nail at the same time being torn from one of them".

The workmen certainly chose a bad time to unload building materials. The building took place in the autumn and, on the first Wednesday in September, the temperature on Wivenhoe Quay was estimated to be, by the local newspaper, 121°F, while in October it was still registering 110°F.

Sir Claude having gone, the Corsellis family returned to Wivenhoe Hall and were not so keen on the noise of the trains or on the construction of the new Station. A fence was put up in the summer to protect the Hall from the noise - and part of it was blown down in a bad storm the following November.

In 1882 the Great Eastern began to evolve a standard colour scheme for its engines to balance the great variety of shades and colours that had gone before. Trains on the Branch would be hauled by smart royal blue engines with wide black edging and red lining. The letters G.E.R. in gold leaf and shading adorned the sides of the tenders. Freight and tank engines were black lined in red and this colour scheme endured until the Great War.

The Great Eastern, after a lot of criticism, was beginning to live up to the word 'Great'. The Eastern Counties had often been mocked for its inefficiency, unpunctuality and easy-going attitude and the Great Eastern seemed, at first, to follow this trend, but now it was starting to get a grip on the situation. The James Holden locomotive era was beginning and it seemed, as was to be proved, that nothing could withstand the Great Eastern in this part of England.

For the Brightlingsea line itself, while other railways in the country lost some of their initial prosperity, the 1880s were good years. Shares were paying good dividends, the Chairman stating on 22nd February, 1886, that "While   almost every railway was, as compared to other years, in an unsatisfactory condition, the success of the Wivenhoe and Brightlingsea Railway had never been so great or the general outlook so bright".

He had every reason to be pleased. Figures for shellfish and sprats carried during 1882-5 show the profitability of the line and shows that the hoped-for sprat trade was beginning to be realised

SHELLFISH		SPRATS	
1882	1,700 tons	107 tons
1883	2,000 tons	695 tons
1884	2,100 tons	649 tons
1885	2,600 tons	807 tons

To give an idea of the oyster prosperity: after a five or six week trip, the Brightlingsea boat *Guide* brought back 49,000 oysters in 1887.

The Colchester to Wivenhoe section of the line was doubled between 1884 and 1886 and the small section from Thorpe-le-Soken was completed in 1882.

The next move by the over-shadowing Great Eastern was to take over the Tendring Hundred railway on 1st July, 1883. It was all looking rather dangerous: there were now few branch lines left that were not Great Eastern owned, but the Brightlingsea Line remained fiercely independent, even if it had lost its *Resolute*.

Population figures for Brightlingsea had risen to 3,443 in 1881, justifying the Railway and, in the following year, came the raised Causeway at Brightlingsea Hard which, following the failure of Bradley's Quay, became the landing

Brightlingsea Hard. The station buildings can be seen in the top left (*Real Photos*)

place for sprats. Sprat landings were at an all-time high. In the winter of 1885, one boat, *Test*, owned by John French, netted 2,300 bushels (57½ tons) in one try. These were, with the help of the Railway, caught, sold, delivered and paid for all within one week. Oyster totals were often 2,000 tons, all leaving Brightlingsea for an eager London market.

In 1887 the *Royal* Hotel opened in New Street and an advertisement said that their porter attended every train and, as an additional attraction: "Wild-fowl have arrived in the local marshes. Steam and sailing boats with Large guns are available for the accommodation of visitors". Wildfowl there might have been, but nothing will ever beat the great rabbit catching scheme reported in the Brightlingsea *Parish Magazine* of October, 1886.

Passengers travelling by night, either in total darkness or holding candle lanterns, noticed eerie lights flitting to and fro as the train crossed the great curve of the Brightlingsea Marsh. The reason was certainly the most unusual method of netting rabbits ever recorded. Poachers placed lighted candles on the backs of crabs they had caught from the creeks and sent them down the rabbit holes, where they were doubtless eager to go to escape from their captors. It was hoped that the flickering lights corning towards them would be too much for the rabbits, who would make a hasty exit from another hole, only to run straight into the poachers' nets. The writer of the article adds that this method had not proved very successful; possibly, he

supposed, the rabbits became used to these happenings and so lay in wait... and blew the candles out!

Although there is no connection with this last story, the line was becoming known as 'the Crab and Winkle'. This seems hardly appropriate to the freight, but pet names were given to many branch lines and this was not the only 'crab and winkle' line in England. There was a 'cockle and shrimp' line not too far away and, in the Midlands, one was even nicknamed the 'cheese and onion', possibly because this was the favoured contents of the driver's sandwiches. Once adopted, the term 'crab and winkle' was to remain for the lifetime of the branch.

The line seems to have withstood England's worst earthquake of Tuesday, 22nd April, 1884, which, at 9.18 a.m., caused so much damage to Wivenhoe and the surrounding area. There is no mention of damage to the track, but at Colchester Station a locomotive was thrown so hard against the side of the platform that hot coals fell out of the cab, and from there to Wivenhoe the line was closed for the rest of the day and presumably for some time afterwards, as the Great Eastern, following repairs, refused to run passenger trains until a heavy locomotive had been driven across all the bridges and track.

Whether the line did, in fact, need to be repaired following the earthquake is not known, but it continued on its prosperous way for several years, with the Great Eastern keeping an ever-watchful eye on the line it wanted to gain. Now it decided to play another game - one it had not lost yet.

During the time of the W & B R C's independence, the G.E.R. suddenly announced that trains of the Wivenhoe and Brightlingsea Company could no longer use Great Eastern owned track and so trains from Brightlingsea would have to stop some 200 yards short of Wivenhoe Station to which passengers had to walk if they wished to catch a connecting train.

Two temporary platforms were erected near Elsie Cottages in Paget Road, one 110 feet long on the Paget Road side (the road went no further than the railway) and the other 75 feet long. The Company were going to try to beat the clever plan that had forced other lines to sell out to the Great Eastern, and there was a clause in the original contract permitting them to do just that.

Passengers would have been unhappy about the walk, but could do so if necessary; but freight would have to be carried from one train to the other and with 2,000 tons of oysters a year, not to mention the sprats, it would be very difficult. Sidings were built by the W & B R C to try to remedy the situation of the freight transportation, but then... the sprat harvests failed!

In the winters of 1891 and 1892 the sprats just never came. The men of Brightlingsea who worked as crewmen on the large yachts all summer and on the sprat boats in the winter found themselves quickly without money and the railway faced a huge reduction in freight traffic.

For the people of Brightlingsea some

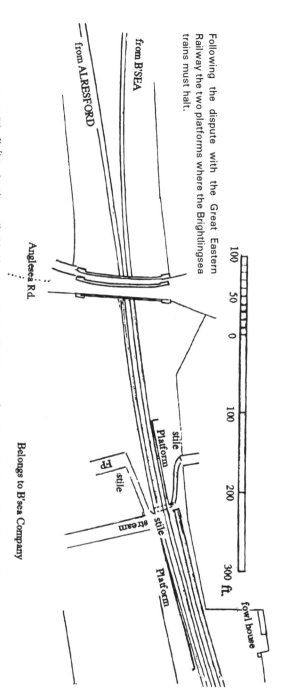

kind of help was given. An eccentric American millionaire, Bayard Brown, whose yacht the *Valfreya* was moored in Brightlingsea Creek, gave £50 to Canon Pertwee, the local rector, to distribute among the local men who had large families to care for. Canon Pertwee was one of those people who become a legend in their own lifetime: he would shelter children coming home from school on rainy evenings under the big coat that he wore, often walking along with many smaller legs trotting beside his. Without making a great show of his generosity, children whose fathers had fallen on hard times would find the 'Vicar's sandwich' being pressed secretively into their hands. This consisted of a sixpenny piece between two halfpennies. On stormy nights the light in the trees, seen by the train passengers as the train crossed the marsh, was a storm lantern placed at the top of the church tower by Canon Pertwee to guide the ships home to the River Colne and safety.

Relief for the needy there may have been, but none for the line. The situation was impossible and, even before the bad sprat harvests, the sale of the line to the Great Eastern had been foreseen. The *Parish Magazine* of July, 1891, stated "One of the best pieces of news we have heard for a long time is that at last the Wivenhoe and Brightlingsea Railway has at length become the property of the Great Eastern. We trust we may now look for some improvements which have long been desired in that connection. First and foremost of which is a new Station". Despite the addition of various offices and buildings to the original Station ten years before, it was still hated. Standing on a winter's day in an open barn on the marshland with narrow platforms and no waiting room, the Station had been disliked by the locals from the day the line opened.

In January, 1893, the sale price of £31,000 was agreed upon and on 1st August the Wivenhoe and Brightlingsea

The steam yacht *Valfreya*, home of the American millionaire, Bayard Brown.

Railway Company slipped into history to join the ghosts of many others that had been seen since the first days of steam.

All this passed unnoticed by the Wivenhoe people who were probably far more interested in watching the Boxing Baboon, the star attraction of the Bank Holiday Fête in Wivenhoe Park.

The winter following the take-over, the sprats came again. The caring and well-loved Canon was able to report from Brightlingsea Hard, "Sprats are what we chiefly think of, talk of and smell sprats of."

The platforms put up in their last ditch stand by the Wivenhoe and Brightlingsea remained there for many years afterwards. Those on the Paget Road side always seemed to young children to be a stage specially erected or their benefit. 'Dancing' and 'Concerts' were held here almost every night, as young girls spun round and round imagining themselves to be the latest London Music Hall sensation.

The boys had other ideas and would remove planks for their games of 'pirates' or, in later days, 'gangsters', but the girls would always find replacements. Eventually the 'Stage' grew more and more derelict as the planks slowly vanished. The cause - not the little boys or woodworm, the Wivenhoe people burnt it all as firewood at the start of the Depression Years.

The signal box, built in 1886, on Wivenhoe Station. The postcard was published in 1910

The Great Eastern did nothing to improve Brightlingsea Railway Station, which was to become the subject of much ill humour for the coming years. If nothing else, its violent condemnation livened Parish Council Meetings and, in the pubs, would have made the third topic of conversation following the ever-popular yarns of sprats and yacht races.

One of the first moves that the new owner carried out was in July, 1898, when the line was doubled between Wivenhoe and Great Bentley. The Brightlingsea Branch remained single as it ran either on a narrow trackbed next to the Marsh, through woodland with trees almost touching the carriages, or over the single track Swing Bridge.

With the doubling of the Bentley line a new signal box was provided from July, 1898, at Wivenhoe Junction where the lines to Brightlingsea and to Alresford parted. Situated on a raised piece of ground between the two parting tracks it had a rather interesting appearance, Mr Orme of the Great Eastern Railway Society describes "Something of a cliff-hanger was the small squat Wivenhoe Junction Box, perched as it was on the brink of the grassy mound beneath it. Constructed with the familiar wooden weather boarding of that age, and sitting up there on high, it reminded me of a crooked or haunted house that one often comes across in the middle of an

Through countryside. A train near White House Beach, the Edwardian picnic spot.

amusement park or fairground and, in the Biblical sense, the signalman himself must have appeared as though he had just delivered a 'Sermon on the Mount' when descending the steps to hand over or collect the single line staff, as it was also a Staff Station. I can well recollect the few point rods and signal wires that were to be seen protruding from its base towards the edge, and by means of the usual cranks and pulley wheels, were then directed downwards immediately in front of the earthy face of the mound -

56

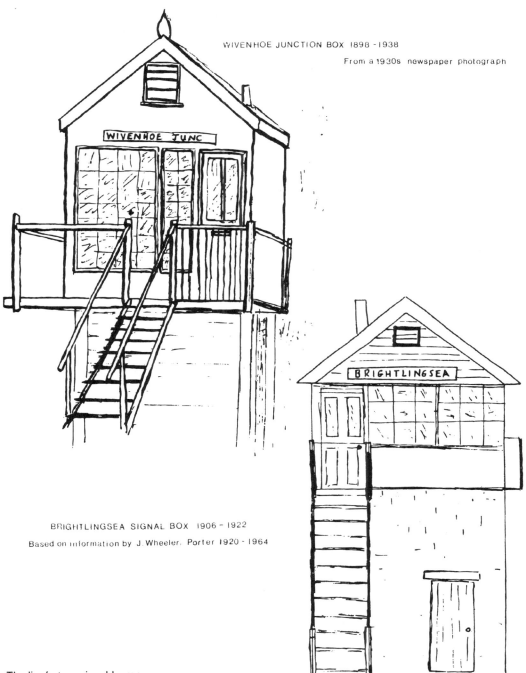

WIVENHOE JUNCTION BOX 1898 - 1938

From a 1930s newspaper photograph

WIVENHOE JUNC

BRIGHTLINGSEA

BRIGHTLINGSEA SIGNAL BOX 1906 - 1922

Based on information by J. Wheeler, Porter 1920 - 1964

The line's two signal-boxes

WEEK DAYS. — **SUNDAYS.**

FROM		
LONDON (Liverpool Street)	dep.	
Chelmsford	,,	
Cambridge	,,	
Sudbury	,,	
Colchester	arr.	
Yarmouth (South Town)	dep.	
Lowestoft	,,	
Norwich (V.)	,,	
Norwich (T.)	,,	
Ipswich	,,	
Colchester	arr.	
COLCHESTER (Main Line)	dep.	
St. Botolph's	,,	
Hythe	,,	
WYVENHOE	,,	
Wyvenhoe	dep.	
BRIGHTLINGSEA	arr.	
Alresford	,,	
Thorington	,,	
Great Bentley	,,	
Weeley	,,	
THORPE	,,	
Thorpe	dep.	
Kirby Cross	,,	
FRINTON-ON-SEA	,,	
WALTON-ON-THE-NAZE	arr.	
WALTON-ON-THE-NAZE	dep.	
FRINTON-ON-SEA	,,	
Kirby Cross	,,	
Thorpe	arr.	
Thorpe	dep.	
CLACTON-ON-SEA	arr.	
CLACTON-ON-SEA	dep.	
Thorpe	arr.	

FROM		
WALTON-ON-THE-NAZE	dep.	
FRINTON-ON-SEA	,,	
Kirby Cross	,,	
Thorpe	,,	
THORPE	dep.	
Weeley	,,	
Great Bentley	,,	
Thorington	,,	
Alresford	,,	
WYVENHOE	dep.	
Hythe	,,	
St. Botolph's	,,	
COLCHESTER (Main Line)	arr.	
Colchester	dep.	
Ipswich	,,	
Norwich (T.)	,,	
Norwich (V.)	,,	
Lowestoft	,,	
Yarmouth (South Town)	arr.	
BRIGHTLINGSEA	dep.	
Wyvenhoe	arr.	
Colchester	dep.	
Sudbury	,,	
Cambridge	,,	
Chelmsford	,,	
LONDON (Liverpool Street)	arr.	

N.T.B.　A On Mondays and Saturdays leave Norwich, Thorpe, at 10.5 a.m.　B On Saturdays arrives at Sudbury at 4.51 p.m.　G To Norwich, Thorpe, on Mondays and Saturdays only.
H Via. Ipswich.　　☞ Horses and Private Carriages not conveyed by these Trains.

The Tendring Hundred timetable for 1896 showing the times of the Brightlingsea trains.

seemingly without much visible means of support - so it was quite a contraption".

The Box opened for service on weekdays from 7.40 a.m. until 7.50 p.m. and on Sundays from 9 until 7.50, unless the Brightlingsea trains passed at some time other than the normal timetable.

The Box at Wivenhoe Station, situated at the Station Road side at the very end of the platform towards Brightlingsea, was replaced by one situated at the other end of the Station, probably during the 1886 rebuilding. Details of the new Station Box and the Junction Box are in Appendix 3.

The 'Staff' mentioned in connection with the Junction Box was a device carried by the driver and, while in his possession, ensured that no other train could come on to the single line track. It was made of brass and inscribed "Brightlingsea and Wivenhoe Junction", but this was not so simple as it may seem and will be described in more detail later.

The timetable was to change as well, with a marked contrast seemingly in favour of London theatre goers. Starting in 1897, the last train from Wivenhoe to Brightlingsea left at 7.40 p.m. on a Saturday. London travellers who had enjoyed a night out on the Town could leave Liverpool Street on a train with a supper buffet at three minutes after midnight, roar through sleeping Wivenhoe at 1.20 a.m., arriving at Clacton 23 minutes later.

This was, no doubt, welcomed by the Stage Door Johnnies of the time, who could, if they wished, spend a quiet Sunday by the sea to return from Clacton on the Monday Breakfast Train at 7.43 a.m. Clacton-on-Sea had now become very popular, but, though most of the track in this area was becoming doubled, the Thorpe-le-Soken to Clacton section remained single until 1941.

During these years it would be more correct, in referring to Wivenhoe, to use the spelling 'Wyvenhoe'. This appeared in the timetables of July, 1879, and then, just as quickly, disappeared after October, 1911.

The Company's engineers, Mr Cooke and Mr Greaves, should have realised that building a railway that would also be a barrier against the sea was a very risky business. Anyone who can still remember the salt spray striking the carriage windows as the train rocked on the track, buffeted by a Force 8 gale, will now how close the line came to serious flooding. From the start of the line the foods came, for the railway had been built on a sea wall above the flat sea marsh and even ran alongside the sea itself in certain places, protected only by piles of rocks. In some places these rocks and ballast, laid down during construction, raised the track no more than a metre above high water mark.

The line had only been open eight years when, in March, 1874, the floods came, an event repeated in the same month of 1876. In the summer of the latter year the sea wall was heightened, but, despite these efforts, a tide of 19th February, 1882, flooded both the Marsh and the Railway and from then on began a battle between sea and railway that was to last nearly a hundred years.

The first flood to be photographed. The view from Anglesea Road bridge, Wivenhoe, in November, 1903

(*Author's collection*)

Brightlingsea Branch flooded Sunday 23/11/03.

The first serious flooding was in 1897. With the high tide due at 3.40 p.m. a train from Colchester, due at Brightlingsea at 2.47 p.m. got to within two hundred yards of the Station, when flood waters prevented it going any further. The ballast had been washed away from under the track and one wagon had been swept from the line. The passengers waited anxiously until they were rescued by rowing boat and brought to the Station, quite a job considering that the dresses of the day were suitable neither for climbing from the train nor sitting in a crowded rowing boat. It was several days before an effective repair could be made and a horse-drawn omnibus service took passengers to Thorrington.

The weather also proved quite capable of halting trains away from the coast. On 18th February, 1881, passengers had to spend a whole night in a train which got stranded in a snow drift between Wivenhoe and Colchester. After a night of darkness and no food, they decided the next morning to try walking to Wivenhoe Station. This was eventually reached, and some struggled on to Brightlingsea.

Floods continued and every few years the local *Parish Magazine* or newspaper reported more chaos as waters swept over the line. On 28th November, 1901, the service was interrupted for several days. On 21st November, 1903, a high tide one Saturday night washed away half a mile of ballast and track. It seems that what-

The train that got through. A locomotive, possibly carrying ballast for the track, approaches Wivenhoe Junction box in November 1903 (*Photo courtesy of John Stewart*)

ever repairs were made they were always insufficient to be any lasting deterrent.

The line served not only Wivenhoe and Brightlingsea residents, but attracted people from quite an area around. Mrs Dawson of West Mersea, having moved from London, found that the journey back to visit her old friends entailed a 12 mile trip to Colchester Station, sitting on the carrier's cart. The situation was solved by a walk to East Mersea Beach and a row across to Navvy Creek, where it was possible to land at Bradley's Quay beside the Station. The Station Master would always stop the train, or the driver would pull back into the Station, if a rowing boat appeared in the mouth of the Creek. In those days, instead of the Station Master's whistle for the train's departure, a bell would be rung. At Brightlingsea, tickets were originally sold from a leather bag carried by one of the station staff, but a booking office window was eventually added to the end of one of the sidings.

Brightlingsea legend, often quoted, is that the channel cutting through Cindrey Island in the Brightlingsea Creek was made by a man from St Osyth who used to row across and catch the train each morning, rowing round the Island to do so. One day, it is said, tiring of this, he decided to cut a gap through to reduce the distance. Sadly, a map of 1841 shows the gap to be there then, but there is some truth in the story, as there often is in these old tales, for it was cut by hand, but in the early 1800s, by a St Osyth man, who, tiring of riding his horse to Brightlingsea, left it tied up on St Osyth Marshes and rowed through the channel he had cut himself. The gap is still there, although erosion now gives the impression of two separate islands.

Not only were the methods of travel to reach the train unorthodox, but also were methods of travel on the train itself. John Leather in *The Northseaman* tells an interesting story of an occurrence about 1900. 'Monkey' Byford, later to become Mastheadman on the *Britannia*, but then a local yachtsman, came to Brightlingsea for two weeks R.N.R. training. He just missed the train at Wivenhoe Station, it was pulling out as he arrived. Not be beaten, he raced after it, grabbed the last buffer and swung on to it, where he hung for the next 5 miles to give himself a free and often-talked-about ride to

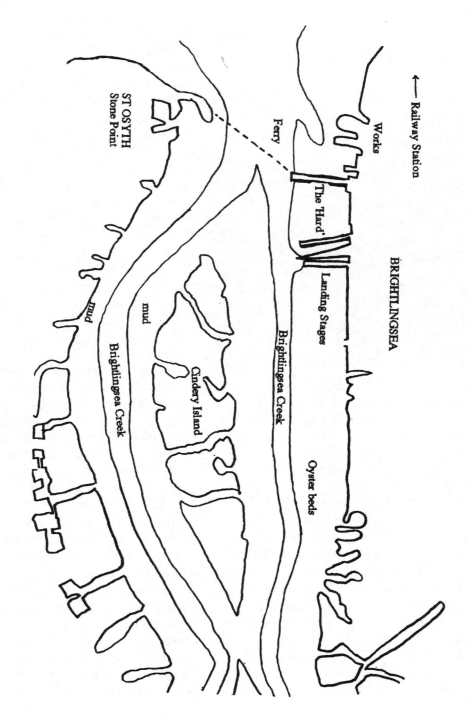

Cindery Island and Ferry Route, Brightlingsea

Brightlingsea.

The Brightlingsea Signal Box in the early days of the line consisted of a simple wooden shed about the size of a small lineside hut, near the end of the platform on the opposite side of the track. It was lightish grey in colour and had windows facing both ways.

When no longer in use it became a platelayers' hut and was found by the station staff to be an ideal place for a quick game of cards. This even continued in later years after the hut had been demolished, as planks at ground level now covered the lever bay and, not only could the card games continue down there (they were usually station staff versus the platelayers), but they were now nicely hidden away from the eyes of the Station Master or Foreman.

Another game was for all the station staff to dash across and hide below the planks - just the job to play havoc with the nerves of any Station Master finding himself suddenly alone on a station with a train due any minute.

Small alterations were carried out to the Station, but little was done to ease the discontent of the passengers. Some alterations were not being done quite officially: Thomas Moy, the coal merchant, erected a building without planning permission and was reprimanded for it by the Parish Council in 1897 (The illustration below is taken from a very faded sepia photograph shows these buildings. This is believed to be the only surviving photograph of the old Station buildings and there is none of the Station itself).

The only photograph of Brightlingsea station taken before the fire of 1901, showing the goods area. Mr Sergeant's horse waits patiently, its cart loaded with oyster barrels, while the three staff pose for a photograph. (*Author's collection*)

It is worth examining this photo in more detail. Not only were Moy's daring enough to put up the buildings without permission, but the vertical board on the roof is probably a large 'Moy' sign facing the Station. A five plank wagon belonging to them is beside the building. The photograph also shows a delivery cart loaded with bags of oysters: these were disliked by the station staff because of their smell, but they had little cause for complaint as a request to load fish manure on the trains had recently been refused by the Council and oysters would have seemed sweet by comparison. The bearded man on the delivery cart is Mr George Cook, in the employ of Mr Sergeant, the agent - whose initial 'S' can be seen on the horses' headbands. On the left is Ted Hills, the goods porter, who left the Station in 1917 to become a guard, a common practice for anyone near retirement. He was replaced by John Wheeler, the man who gave so much information for this book, who remained at the Station until its closure. The building had not been condemned, as the sign on the roof might seem to suggest - old wagon covers, even those that had been condemned, make an excellent substitute for roofing felt.

The Great Eastern had been criticised for poor service. Twice in the autumn of 1897 the first train out had failed to start, leaving many stranded and unhappy passengers on what were, one hopes, mild mornings for one complaint was beginning to outweigh all others.

The discontent over the Station grew from simple dissatisfaction to hatred and it seemed as if the Great Eastern would do nothing about it. They continually promised a new station building, but nothing seemed be done. This was not entirely the G.E.R's fault: the then Lord of the Manor, Mr Pulleyne, was not keen to sell the necessary land. The 'Railway Lords' had now gone for ever.

Not only did the open-ended barn mean cold and misery in the winter, but the narrow and often low-lying crowded platform was very dangerous when a train was shunting by. "Someone three parts tight will have to be killed and then it will be attended to," growled Squire Bateman at an 1897 Council meeting. Although he might have been an unusual man, with his local experiments of tobacco crops and eucalyptus trees, there could have been no-one at the meeting who disagreed with him. "A structure which for squalor, discomfort and inconvenience it would probably be hard to match in the whole of the United Kingdom," declared the Council five years later.

In March, 1898, Doctor Cooper of Brightlingsea decided to take matters into his own hands, following a brief visit to the Station. He wrote to the Great Eastern about the unhealthy state of the line and was assured that plans were being prepared and that something would be done soon - it was !

William Beaumont, the Brightlingsea Engine Cleaner, left home at 11 p.m. on Monday, 30th December, 1901, having enjoyed a late supper. That was the only pleasant part of his night, as the last train would have arrived and the engine would begin to cool. Soon he could start the unenviable task of cleaning out cinders, soot and dust amidst almost suffocating fumes. Rounding a corner of Station Road he met a sight that made him break into a run: the whole station seemed surrounded by a red glow. Rushing on to a platform, Mr Beaumont saw that a carriage was blazing fiercely. There was nothing he could do on his own, so he ran to the engine, which was still in steam, and Brightlingsea was made aware of the fire by shrill blasts of a whistle echoing through the winter's night.

First on the scene was the Station Master, George Ruffell, followed by the local policeman. Seeing that nothing could be done to save the station, to which the fire had spread, Mr Ruffell jumped on to the track and undid the coupling between the burning carriage and that next to the engine. He then boarded the engine and drove it and the undamaged carriage clear of the station.

News of the fire spread through Brightlingsea. "The Station's afire," folk were told and, before long, a crowd eventually to total nearly a hundred appeared and set to work to try to save as much as possible of the mobile station equipment. The wooden station itself could offer no resistance to the fire and, within two hours, all that was left were some twisted ironwork and the remains of some automatic vending machines.

The next day, with the superb control and calmness then customarily connected with the railway, the first train of the morning drew out on schedule and only a scorched end to the one carriage and the fact the passengers were therefore more crowded together than usual bore witness to what had happened the night previous.

The draughty station had gone. In fact, it was this same draught that had helped fan the flames and speed its end. There only remained the 'platelayers' hut', signal box and water tank. The only victim was the Station Master's dog, whose body was found in the charred remains.

The cause of the fire was never determined. Some believed that it did not start in the carriage at all, but in the Porters' Room shortly after the arrival of the train at 8 p.m and that reflection in the carriage windows gave the impression that it had started on the train. Another theory was that the fire was started by a spark from the locomotive which was usually stored under the station roof at night. To me it all seems very simple: the station had been hated by the locals for years. They were constantly promised a new station and never got it. The Lord of the Manor was hindering the G.E.R. in getting the station built. The local doctor had condemned the place as 'unhealthy'. It was now a cold winter, the worst time of year for passengers and the Christmas festivities were at their height. The station was unmanned at the time... It seems the only thing not found out was - who held the match?

That Tuesday was a busy one for the staff; not only was there clearing up to be done, but as many as could be spared were given time off to attend the funeral of David Ainger, a Ticket Clerk, who had worked at the Station since the beginning of the line and died just before its most dramatic event.

That New Year's Eve was not just the ending of the year, but also the end of the first chapter of the history. The Station itself had been burnt down, one of the Station staff, who had always been a part of the line was buried, and even the burnt-out carriage, No. 125, had been a memento of the line's struggle for independence.

As midnight approached people were drawn towards the remains of the Station, where they joined hands in the darkness and sang *Auld Lang Syne*. For them the end of the hated station, for the line it was the end of an era.

A small part of the station was to be used as a goods shed and retained to the end, a reminder of the former days in the form of a small window set into the wall for the issue of tickets from the office.

The floods continued, even during the building of the new Station, which took four years, and the repairs to the sea wall and track made in 1903 were to prove inadequate. One of the most serious floods was on 30th December, 1904, the third anniversary of the Station Fire. That Friday, between six and seven in the evening, driven by a gale that had been raging in the North Sea, the water broke through between the Swing Bridge and Wivenhoe, washing away a mile of track. Flooding had not been expected. Mr Allen, the Station Master at Wivenhoe, stopped the 6.15 train from Colchester, as by now the line beyond the Junction Box had gone. The

A Sunday School outing waits for their train at Thorrington Station in about 1910. (*Author's collection*)

passengers were taken on to Thorrington by train where they were left to walk the three miles home. At Wivenhoe, the Gas Works were partially submerged and the whole of the town's lighting failed, making the job in the two signal boxes very difficult until oil lamps could be fetched. Several pigs were drowned on the Wivenhoe Marshes adjoining the line and gaps had to be cut in the sea wall to allow the water to escape. An unusual feature of the flood was that it happened at the time of the neap tide, when such an event is least likely.

This flood had been the seventh in the line's short history; three in the last four years. Even while engaged in the construction of a complete new station, the Great Eastern looked at this record and decided to abandon the work and close the line, as it was proving a serious financial liability and the danger of a fatal accident could not be ruled out.

A plan, resurrected from some 40 years earlier, was put forward to build a new line to Thorrington and finish with the flooding for ever. Another proposal, that the line be used for goods traffic only, brought violent protests from the local people. Brightlingsea, they argued, got most of its summer finance from people coming into the town for the yachting, and closure of the railway would cause a serious drop in trade.

Three weeks later the line was re-opened. While repairs were in progress, the Great Eastern had provided an often-unpunctual motor bus service to

A Great Eastern omnibus reaching the parts that others cannot reach. One similar to this, photographed at West Mersea, connected St Osyth with Clacton. (*Photo Essex Countryside*)

Thorrington. The rebuilding of the sea wall cost some £200 and the several owners agreed to share with the G.E.R. the cost, not only of reconstruction, but of increase in height. This is the sea wall that runs between Wivenhoe Shipyards and the wood that once contained the railway track. The rebuilding of the wall would be "A good idea to provide work for the Wyvenhoe men during the Winter," the *Gazette* stated.

The repair must have been a job well done, as the next recorded flooding was not until 6/7th January, 1928, when little damage was done to the railway, although 14 people elsewhere were drowned. Perhaps, the sea was giving the line a chance. However, if it was in a cheerful mood, others were not !

The Great Eastern might have had second thoughts on the failure to extend the line to St Osyth, as, in July, 1905, it instituted an omnibus service between St Osyth and Clacton. The buses were red and cream with 'Great Eastern' in dark blue on their sides. The St Osyth service was 'summer only' to provide transport for happy Edwardian holidaymakers who perhaps were not as numerous as expected, for the service closed in the summer of 1907.

The Great Eastern had other new ideas during that period and even considered, in 1903, building a bridge across the River Colne between Wivenhoe and Rowhedge to enable more people to use the trains, despite the two ferries being always well used. Although it came to nothing it was not just wild speculation Wivenhoe Council was still arguing about it in 1937.

The new Station was planned to be an imposing building to the east of the original, away from the Marsh. Permission from the Lord of the Manor was required before work could start, an interesting example of how the power of the Lordship had been maintained for centuries.

The new buildings were to last the life of the railway. Ballast for the station site was brought in trucks from the goods area of St Botolph's Station, which was being enlarged. The transportation of that material over a distance of 8 miles must have been a long and arduous task.

The contractors were W Pattinson & Co of Rushington, who tendered for the

Brightlingsea's new station.

Floppy hats are in this year! A pony and trap with the local lads waits outside Brightlingsea's new station. (*Author's collection*)

The Refreshment Room staff. A posed photograph taken on the station's opening day, 3rd September, 1906 (*Author's collection*)

new station and loco facilities (sheds) for the sum of £12,053 and, in early June, 1906, McKensie & Holland of Worcester were given the order for the new signal box. Pattinson did his job well and cheaply, the final cost of the station buildings being £7,130, £1,790 less than the original tender. It was hoped to appease locals by providing a Refreshment Room in the station buildings: the 'automatic vending machines', the only things that had been recognisable after the fire, would no longer be needed.

The Station was completed for opening on Monday, 3rd September, 1906, and passengers no longer had to stand and wait for the trains as, in addition to the Waiting Room, six station seats were provided, one of which still 'lives on' in my garden.

The first train out from the new station at Brightlingsea. A photograph taken from the base of the signal box. They have not even had time to put a sleeve on the water column. (*Author's collection*)

On that Monday there was no great ceremony. Perhaps the only important person was the local photographer eager to try out his new press camera, who made an excellent record of it all, even photographing two ladies serving the refreshments.

It appears that the Station was opened in a hurry, for the photograph of the first train to leave shows the water column, of L.N.W.R. pattern not Great Eastern, lacking a delivery pipe.

The first locomotive out was an Intermediate T26 2-4-0 tender loco (later L.N.E.R. Class E4), one of which is preserved in the Railway Museum at York. There is no certainty for what period this type of engine ran on the line, as no records exist. They were painted black with red lining and were used for main line traffic from their introduction in 1891 until superseded by the Claud Hamilton Class 4-4-0s (named after a G.E.R. director) and for many years the 'Intermediates' were the pride of the railways, when they became a familiar sight on cross-country and branch lines, the last of the Class surviving until 1960. One of the locomotives that ran on the Line, Number 466, shows the soundness of their design and construction: built in 1892, she survived until 1954.

A Class E4. The first locomotive to serve the new Brightlingsea Station. (*Photo R. E. Batten*)

Earlier that month the excitement of the new Station was possibly too much for one lad named Selby who, finding a fog detonator on the marshes near the Station, threw it to the ground to see what would happen - and was admitted to Colchester Hospital with injuries to his face and hands.

Even after the Station opening, the G.E.R. was unhappy about the line, especially as so much had been spent on the Station. Cheap fares, as offered for other seaside towns, proved unsuccessful and were discontinued and repeated applications by the Brightlingsea Council for their re-instatement were refused.

The Station built, the floods gone (for a while at least), the line settled to a few years of peace in the Edwardian summers before the Great War.

On the Wivenhoe Marshland, by a small sandy beach near Alresford Creek, where once stood Copyhold Farm, there now stood a small white house that looked more like a cottage, but even so, the beach was named White House Beach. Both the generosity of the people living there and the kindness of the station staff at Wivenhoe made it a favourite picnic spot. The staff would, if you happened to know one well - or to be an attractive young lady, have a word with the driver, who would halt the train there while Papa, Mama and the children, complete with picnic hamper, made a 'jump for it' for a day on the beach. On its return the train would stop at the wave of a hand and a gallant gentleman would climb up quite a distance to the carriage, open the door,

71

Edwardian hey-days. Near the curve where the train coming from Wivenhoe enters the woods.

The white disk on the funnel shows it to be an ordinary passenger train. S44 No 1121 at Brightlingsea.

and then help the others aboard. To help the picnic along, the owners of the White House would always boil a kettle for tea.

The picnics would be interspersed with whistles of passing trains, as there was a rather complex 'whistle system' in operation at that time. The trains on the main line had only to whistle once at a signal, but the branch line gave three blasts on approaching Wivenhoe Junction Box from either direction as an indication that the branch was going to be used or was about to be cleared. A speed limit of 25 miles per hour prevailed between Wivenhoe Station and the Junction Box and the trains from Brightlingsea nearing the Junction were required to stop at the Home Signal whether it was clear or not. The locomotives would all carry a white disc below the funnel, the mark of an ordinary passenger train, that was replaced at night by a white light.

Derailments were not unknown to the branch, but, at least, this now meant a better wait for the passengers on Brightlingsea Station than before. Just as well, as these sometimes took quite a while to put right. On 8th December, 1909, when the 5.43 p.m. was derailed, passengers had to wait until 7.30 for their train to depart. Thank goodness for the Refreshment Room!

As well as helping out in time of flooding, Thorrington Station was to be invaluable for passengers on Sundays. A 'brake' (a large wagonette) would run from Brightlingsea to Thorrington to connect with the 6 p.m. train to London. The fare for this service was 3/6d.

Alternatives to trains were not the only extra service provided: special trains were frequent. Some took passengers on a day's excursion, but when Music Hall was at its most popular, a late Saturday train was put on for returning patrons of

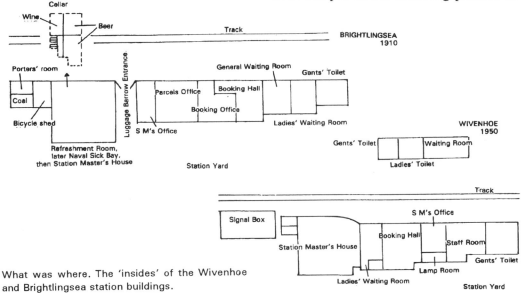

What was where. The 'insides' of the Wivenhoe and Brightlingsea station buildings.

the Colchester *Hippodrome*. This certainly was a late train for the area, leaving St Botolph's at 10.50 p.m. and Wivenhoe at 11: clearly not the most popular train with engine drivers!

It was this train that offers the saddest human story of the line. On Saturday night, 23rd April, 1909, Lily Wade, aged 15, visited the *Hippodrome* for the first time, accompanied by a friend; a special outing for which she had obtained her father's permission. On the return journey they arrived late at St Botolph's and were bundled into a compartment full of Brightlingsea lads who had spent half the evening at the *Hippodrome*, then going to drink shandy in the local pubs. By the time the train reached Wivenhoe, Lily had struck up a friendship with one of the boys and finished the journey sitting on his knee. Instead of joining her friend when they got off the train at Wivenhoe Station, she stood on the platform and chatted to him before the train left. As it did he grasped Lily's hand for a joke to make her run along beside him and, as the train gathered speed, she was dragged rather than pulled. Bert Exworth, the Wivenhoe Junction signalman, who was seeing the train out, grabbed hold of her with his left hand as he held a lamp in his right. She was now screaming, "Look at him! Look at him!" As they neared the end of the platform, the lad suddenly let go and they fell between the platform and the train. The wheels ran over Lily's legs and Mr Exworth, who only had cuts to his face, called for the local doctor, who was brought at once. On Doctor Squire's arrival, Lily was carried to a wagonette and placed on the bottom, while Dr Squire and Police Sergeant Lancum sat on either side of her. The cart was driven as fast as possible to Colchester Hospital, where it was decided not to operate as the wounds were so bad. Lily died on Monday evening.

At the Coroner's Inquest not only was Bert Exworth congratulated, but so too should have been the friends of the Brightlingsea boy who held Lily's hand. It was not his hand that Lily held at all, some of them said, but a handkerchief, and others, a carriage window. The Coroner, however, guessed what it had all been about and recorded a verdict of accidental death, giving a warning of the dangers of playing with trains. Lily was buried in the new Wivenhoe Cemetery one week later. The Rev Sinclaire Carolin remarked in his funeral address how she had been singing in the Church just a week before her death, but now she was a member of the 'Celestial Choir'. The local press by contrast, having not yet freed itself from the love of morbid details, described the hunt at Brightlingsea Station for skin on the engine wheels.

Only two engines that ran on the line from its opening have been mentioned so far - *Resolute* and the *Intermediate*. Others have to be, in some part, the result of guesswork, but the following is as near as it is possible to get. For the enthusiast and the model-maker I have put a list in the appendices at the end of this book.

The locomotives running on the line

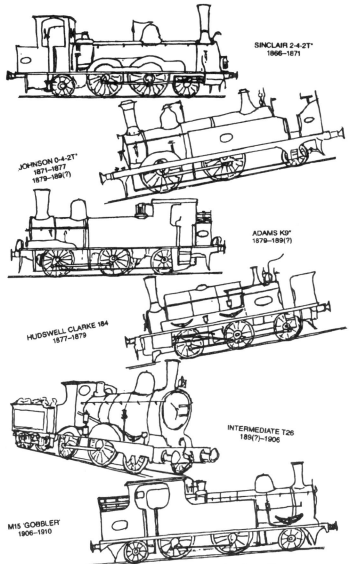

SINCLAIR 2-4-2T*
1866–1871

JOHNSON 0-4-2T*
1871–1877
1879–189(?)

ADAMS K9*
1879–189(?)

HUDSWELL CLARKE 184
1877–1879

INTERMEDIATE T26
189(?)–1906

M15 'GOBBLER'
1906–1910

* = Uncertain as to whether these trains ran on the Brightlingsea Line.

The locomotives that ran the line during the days
of steam.

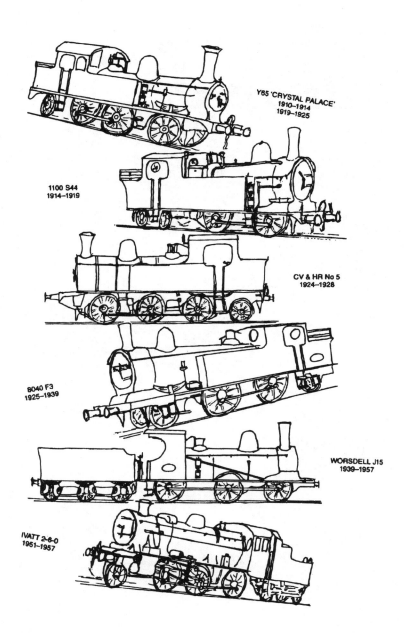

Y65 'CRYSTAL PALACE'
1910–1914
1919–1925

1100 S44
1914–1919

CV & HR No 5
1924–1928

8040 F3
1925–1939

WORSDELL J15
1939–1957

IVATT 2-6-0
1951–1957

before 1910, when the late Langley Aldrich wrote down details of all of them, have to be rather speculative, but as mentioned above there are two exceptions. First, we have photographic evidence of the Great Eastern T26, intermediate leaving the Station on its opening day: sadly the number cannot be seen. Second, from its early history, the W & B R C's own locomotive *Resolute* ran on the line from 1876 in maroon livery and might have continued to do so after the G.E.R. takeover of 1879 and, if it had not been found too light for its work as has been suspected, could have continued until its withdrawal in 1888.

Prior to this one of Robert Sinclaire's locomotives would have been used, possibly the 2-4-2T passenger tank engines first built in 1864, as the driving wheels on the other Sinclaire locomotives seem too big. Chris Jolly, the old engine driver, used to talk of the old Sinclaire Singles, those with a big single driving wheel, but he never mentioned their running on the line.

The most probable locomotives used from the 1870s onwards would be Samuel Johnson's 0-4-2T class T7 light branch engines. Johnson was Locomotive Superintendent for the G.E.R. from 1866 to 1873. Some of the T7s during the designer's period of office were painted chrome yellow, while the earlier locomotives of the Eastern Counties Railway and earlier Great Eastern were, as has been mentioned, light green with chocolate frames. In 1882 the Great Eastern blue livery became the standard colour scheme. Add to this the maroon of *Resolute* and it seems a pity that the only colour most of us remember in this area is a dirty black - and even that was stained with chemical splashes. All these colours must have looked splendid going across the marsh land on a sunny day. One rather hopes that it was not the T7s, with the wide cabs, that ran on this Marsh-land Railway, as they would have been very cold for any winter work. Another

Samuel Johnson's Class T7 locomotive, which ran on the line from 1871 until 1877, when the W.& B.R.C. tried to become independent with its own locomotive *Resolute*

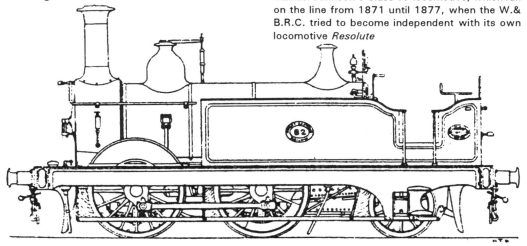

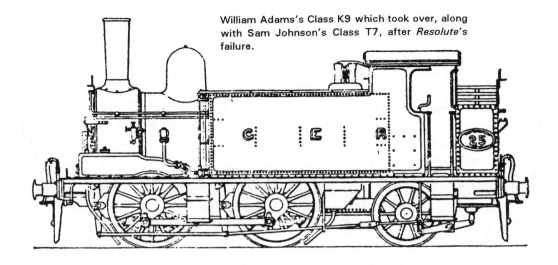

William Adams's Class K9 which took over, along with Sam Johnson's Class T7, after *Resolute's* failure.

'possible' during this period would be William Adam's 0-4-2T Class K9.

When the T7s disappeared between 1891 and 1894, as the Class T26 *Intermediate* were first built in 1891, they presumably took over where the T7s left off, and were to continue on the line until phased out before 1910 by the M 15 2-4-2T *Gobblers* recalled by Langley Aldrich. These locomotives, designed by James Holden, the man who brought to the G.E.R. a sense of purpose with good locomotives and good leadership, got the nick name *Gobbler* due to their high coal consumption.

To the uninitiated who may not understand all these strange references to 2-4-2T, 0-4-2T and so on, it is simple the number of leading (bogie), driving and cab wheels that a locomotive has. The ˙uffix 'T' shows that the tender was *a* built-in part of the locomotive.

In 1910, if *Gobbler* is not an odd enough sounding name for a locomotive, add to that *Crystal Palace* and you'll get the loco that came to replace the *Gobblers. Crystal Palace* is yet another nickname, given this time on account of the engine's outsize cab and six large windows, although, despite these large cabs, they were quite lightweight. Their official designation was Class Y65 2-4-2T and, once again, they were designed by a Holden, but this time James's son, Stephen. These locomotives were especially smart with their Great Eastern blue livery and, to complete the effect, a gold rim surrounding the chimney. It seemed as if they took special pride in themselves as, although the last train arrived in Brightlingsea just after 8 p.m., it was the one before that which earned the name *Swanky Seven* as the blue locomotive roared non-stop through Colchester Hythe Station, proud of the fact that it had no passengers to pick up,

The large windows of the *Crystal Palace* locomotive can just be seen as it pulls a long train past Bateman's Tower

as did those for the rest of the day.

They might not have been blue, but a dull black all over. A year before their arrival on the line in 1910 it was decided to paint all G.E.R. locomotives black for economic reasons. It is said that the Director, Lord Claud Hamilton, was so angered by the sight of one of these engines that the idea was promptly dropped and it is unknown if a black locomotive ever got as far as Brightlingsea, at least before the days of nationalisation.

The *Crystal Palace* serving the line was usually Number 1300 and they were certainly put to good use, judging by the amount of carriage being hauled past Bateman's Tower and 'Gandygoose Bay', as the locals called the entrance to Gandergoose Creek.

These locomotives were to stay until the start of the Great War, although they played a part in a war themselves, when 15 were armoured and used for coastal defence work in World War II.

Now, to take a look at the rolling stock these locomotives pulled. I am grateful to members of the Great Eastern Railway Society for information about locomotives and rolling stock. John Watling of the Society suggests that up to the early years of the century four-wheeled carriages, the type pulled by *Resolute*, would have been used on the line. O S Nock, the railway historian, gives a description of these carriages. "The Firsts were quite luxurious in their seating, although they rode rather hard. The Seconds were much more cramped and although having cushioned seats were straight backed and gave little room for the knees. The Thirds sat on bare boards and the partition extended to shoulder height; one could, if you so wished, climb from one section to another."

There were no restrictions, however, on six wheeled carriages running on the track and any train that came directly from London would probably be made up of these six wheeler stock. They were certainly to be the only stock by 1910.

The usual number of carriages hauled by the *Gobblers* at this time was 5 six wheeler coaches, lit by a naked gas flame enclosed in a glass bowl: in addition to these flames, they often contained rain water and a few dead flies. At dusk it was gripping to watch one of the station staff clamber along the carriage roofs with an oil flare lighting up the lamps. He did not get down at the end of each coach, but jumped from one to the next. Small boys watched, secretly hoping that he would fall - but he never did.

Of course, this was very satisfactory if you were sitting at the end of the train where the gas was first lit, but by the time the other end was reached there was either a very loud 'pop' when it ignited or else a very strong smell of gas beforehand.

The goods wagons used at that time - and for much of the future use of the Line - often bore the name of the company owning them. This could be seen on the sides of the wagons in large white letters with black shading, usually on a grey background, but later on red oxide. Local examples were Thomas Moy, coal merchants of Colchester, the wagons simply having the name 'Moy' on the side; Coote & Warren of Ipswich; and Death, the local Brightlingsea coal merchant.

The line's freight seemed to be the subject of special mention by the G.E.R. In 1910 mixed trains on the line, that is, trains carrying both passengers and freight, were permitted to carry, along with other articles, paraffin, petrol, safety and lucifer matches, and cylinders containing compressed gas and these were also permitted to be carried in 'dumb' or unsprung trucks. What a fire would have done to that collection could only be imagined: perhaps the reason that the line had special permission to carry these was that it was situated near the sea - it gave the crew somewhere to jump!

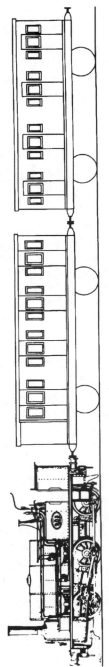

This is how she looked - *Resolute* re-united with her two carriages.

At the start of the War a larger engine appeared on the Line, replacing the *Crystal Palaces*. These were 0-4-4 engines of the 1100 Class (S44). Used to hauling the heavier traffic of the G.E.R. they were mainly used in the London area, but occasionally one or two of them would be able to escape to the Brightlingsea or Clacton branch lines for a breath of seaside air. The usual visitors were Numbers 1121 and 1122 and both engines were shedded at Colchester for the duration of the War.

Now, with wartime austerity, the smart blue livery was changed to battleship grey: the drab paint that most of the region's engines were inflicted with during the war years became a regularly used colour on less important engines until 1927. The only break in the dull grey was the letters 'G.E.R.' in unshaded yellow on the tender sides.

No 1121 of Class S44 standing at Brightlingsea station with the 6 p.m. train, 3rd August, 1919.

WARS AND RUMOURS OF WAR

Along with the new engines came the men who were to prepare for the battle-fields of Flanders. First, on 1st December, 1914, came two companies of the South Midland Divisional Engineers, later in the War, Commonwealth troops from Australia, Canada and New Zealand all arrived in Brightlingsea. Although many of these troops were billeted in a large camp on Brightlingsea Recreation Ground, another gift of Bayard Brown (this camp even having its own butcher's shop), many were housed in the town itself. Any house that was available was used, the only rule being that there had to be a husband in the house before it was selected. When this housing scheme started a Sergeant went through the town, chalking the number of men to be billeted on the front door of each house. The local people were pleased with their new visitors, as part of their training involved the setting up of a new pontoon bridge across Alresford Creek, resulting in a shorter walk from 'Brittlesea' to 'Wivna' and one no longer had to run nervously over the Swing Bridge, constantly looking behind to see if a train was coming. Only once, as a boy, did I have to lie on the flat sides of the bridge as the train passed by, breathing in hard as it passed and thinking that my heart could not beat any louder: it is not the sort of thing you would like to try twice.

As the War, which was going to be all over by Christmas, 1914, wasn't, and the rains and snows of 1917 made all established forms of warfare obsolete, the Brightlingsea marshland was able to provide the correct training facilities for Passchendaele and the Somme; "Water filled creeks of grey mud" came the assessment of the war area and so, for training, the local marshland was used and straight creeks, instead of the usual meandering maze of saltwater channels, show to this day where men prepared themselves for the morning when they would leave Brightlingsea Station with so many others, clutching their kit bags, before starting their journey to Southampton to find the reality of what had been so well concealed by the press and picture magazines.

Recent excavations in the Noah's Ark area have revealed underground tunnels and a large dug-out latrine.

The bridge building helped in other areas besides Brightlingsea. Margaret Leather writes in *Saltwater Village* of a wooden trestle bridge over the Colne from Wivenhoe to Rowhedge enabling troops and guns to pass across without having to go via Colchester. Formally opened by King George V on a visit to Wivenhoe in April, 1916, it seems a shame that the G.E.R. didn't make it into the passenger bridge they had always wanted.

Above all, it was the 'Aussies' who

King George V at the opening of the Rowhedge Bridge (*Photo Miss Jones*)

made the greatest impact on the Railway and Brightlingsea during the War and 'impact' is a carefully chosen word. Court cases and reports of their many activities filled the local papers and it seems that if there was a bit of adventure to be had or a joke to be played, the Australians would be up to it.

All the trains to Colchester in the evening would be stopped at Wivenhoe for quite a while, during which lengthy inspections of tickets were carried out, as so many soldiers tended to 'forget' to buy one as they clambered aboard the train at Brightlingsea.

During the cuts in train services towards the end of the War, when the last train back to Brightlingsea was the 6.38 p.m., the soldiers would 'borrow' the hand trolley usually used by railway workers. This truck consisted of a wheel which, when turned, drove side wheels and propelled the vehicle. This was later to be replaced by a far superior version that ran on the line until its closure, ferrying workmen back and forth. The new vehicle was like a truck with no sides and was moved by means of a two-handled bar mechanism in the centre worked up and down by men standing on either side. Quite high speed could be reached by this action and workmen always had it going as fast as possible, as did the 'Aussies' on their trips home.

The truck was always being stolen for free rides and, after the troops had left, young boys followed their example. Wivenhoe and Brightlingsea station staff would often find it missing on Monday mornings following a spell spent by the

83

local children running it up and down the line.

In preparation for the Hun's expected invasion, Mr Wheeler, the young Brightlingsea porter, was sent to defend the Swing Bridge at night, just in case anybody should come and blow it up. The nights were long, cold and eerie, with often only the calling of the sea birds for company. He would be shaken into life by the sudden bump of the Water Police's boat when they came to check if he was all right. The Water Police were to come under the control of Colchester Corporation in later years, being used for catching oyster thieves. The bridge was never blown up; the only 'action' Brightlingsea saw was when the Wooden Bridge caught fire at 2 p.m. on Whit Monday, 1915. The Wooden Bridge was a trestle bridge about a mile from Brightlingsea Station. Wivenhoe Station was unable to be contacted and the driver noticed a large column of black smoke as his train approached the bridge from the

In those days the marshes went right up to the wooden bridge in the early years of the railway (*From a photograph courtesy of Peter Fisher*)

marshland. The train was halted and the passengers had to dismount and walk to their destination. The Brightlingsea Station Master, Mr Ruffell, sent his staff to deal with the fire and summoned the nearest railway fire engine from Ipswich, 22 miles away. By the time it arrived the fire had been put out and normal train service was resumed at 6 p.m. Although probably started by a cinder, the Brightlingsea people, their heads filled with 'Wars and rumours of wars' were sure it was started by an explosion as "There was so much smoke".

During the War the Brightlingsea Station Refreshment Room closed for ever. There were two reasons for this. Firstly the food shortage - a pity as hot drinks would have been welcomed by the departing troops - and, secondly, it was to be used as an emergency hospital for the war wounded and a naval sick bay. It was never used, except for local sick cases, and after the war, became part of the Stationmaster's house.

It was probably Brightlingsea's usefulness to the Navy that kept the Station open and fully manned during the War. Many smaller stations were closed in May, 1915, the railwaymen having gone to the front. The Brightlingsea Coastguard Patrol ceased with the call-up and was never re-formed.

This allocation of men to the front was to mean altered timetables by January, 1917, not only for the line, but for the whole of Britain. Passenger fares were increased by 50% in an attempt to cut rail travel to the essentials. The fare from Brightlingsea to St Botolph's was

Troops waiting for the train at Great Bentley station before overseas service in World War One
(*Photo Essex Countryside*)

raised from 1/5d to 2/1½d, almost as much as at the close of the line, and that from Brightlingsea to Liverpool Street from 5/3½d to 7/11d. The maximum amount of baggage per person was restricted to 100 lbs, in that age of hat boxes and trunks still a very generous amount. For the soldiers returning home on leave for a brief respite from the mud, rats and death, the fare of the journey home had to be paid by themselves - there was a free pass for the journey back!

In May, 1918, services were cut even more, down to 4 trains each way per day, rather like at the start of the line. The first left Wivenhoe at 8 a.m., the last ran from Brightlingsea at 7.10 p.m. No wonder the 'Aussies' stole the trolley. The 11.22 a.m. train from Wivenhoe was a connection for the 7.20 a.m. Parliamentary Train from London - if anybody had the stamina needed for such a journey! These services were for passenger trains and were still listed under Tendring Hundred Lines in the timetable.

The station at Brightlingsea was still very busy with troop trains and coal trains supplying the drifters and minesweepers in Brightlingsea Creek: these often numbered so many that they stretched to the end of the Goods Yard.

In May, 1918, permission was granted by Brightlingsea Council for a light railway to be constructed on Brightlingsea Hard in connection with troop training. Possibly the end of the War, some six months later, stopped the project ever being completed.

While every industry in the town was receiving news of one of their former employees being killed in action, in September, 1918, came news of the death of Alfred Annis, a former porter who had once served on Brightlingsea Station.

A blackout was imposed on the town with the heat of Zeppelin raids and the ocomotives were fitted with a tarpaulin sheet that ran across a rail fitted to the

85

front of the tender. At least now the railwaymen, spared the horrors of the front, kept warmer in the winter that froze the soldiers in France.

The 'Aussies' were to stay in Brightlingsea until the War's end, enjoying a love/hate relationship with the locals. This seemed to alternate between violent brawls, stealing, and yet holding very entertaining concerts weekly for the inhabitants in the Empire Theatre close to the railway station. These concerts included a wide range of variety about as differing as the troops' behaviour. Patriotic songs were sung, but there were also many 'in' jokes and sketches about the Land of the Kangaroo and the Abbo, that must have left most of the audience wondering what it was all about while the soldiers rolled about in mirth.

At last, in November, 1918, the war ended. The Australians gave a farewell party with dancing all night long in John Street, formerly Hogg Lane. One soldier went and bought up all the fish and chips from a High Street shop and gave them to the crowd. This shop was always well frequented, sometimes too much so and the owner, a Londoner, when things got too much for him, would simply walk out of the shop and into a near-by pub, where he often had to be searched for, found, and dragged back by the hungry customers.

Before the 'Aussies' finally went home one little matter had to be sorted out. During the War much pilfering of Army supplies had been carried out by the Brightlingsea people. Blankets had somehow disappeared along with good

service boots and other articles. The Aussies came to a simple agreement. A hand cart would be sent round the streets and, so it was announced, everything that you had belonging to the Australian Forces that you did not want, put it in the cart and no more would be said about it. As the cart went along a certain street in Brightlingsea a young girl rushed out of a house and carefully placed two babies amongst the other articles.

The railway was to be used as well for some rather pointed comments. If a woman was pregnant yet again, someone would be sure to say, "Well, you know why that is, don't ya? Her husband didn't get off at Wivna."

The War to end Wars was over and finished. Those that came home, came home. Those who could not have their graves abroad and a memorial in the centre of Brightlingsea or in Wivenhoe churchyard.

As a short postscript to the First World War: I have hardly ever heard of it doing anybody any good, at least for the men who were sent to the front, though Fred Scales, who before the War worked for Death, the coal merchant,

Mr Scales, on the right, who was able to buy out his boss, Mr Death, the other man in the photograph, when he received his back pay at the end of the Great War.

was, after the War, when he received his long awaited back pay, able to buy out his former employer and to have two private coal wagons of his own. These wagons, six plankers, displayed his name in white on a grey background.

After the War, another local coal merchant employed a man and a woman, a brother and sister from Lowestoft, to load the coal into bags and take it round the town. Mr Wheeler's comment on the sister: "She was tall and liked a joke, one of those sort!"

If these coal trucks were not cleared out within three days of their arrival at Brightlingsea, there was an increasing fine, known as demurrage, to be paid to the Railway Company. Things often got very close to the given time, resulting in Mr Scales and his two youngest daughters shovelling the coal as hard as they could out of the wagon and on to the ground. There was no charge for coal on the ground!

In 1919 the Clacton & District Omnibus Company decided to set up a

Alternative transport. The 'Silver Queen' char-à-banc prepares to leave Clacton for Brightlingsea in the 1920's, with a happy crew. Maximum speed 12 mph, journey time one hour!

The 'Swiftsure' broken down on All Saints Hill, Brightlingsea. Have the seats been cut from a theatre? Brightlingsea Station, 1920

service in opposition to the railway, running between Brightlingsea and Colchester on Mondays and Thursdays. The journey took one hour and cost three shillings return or two shillings single. No matter how many customers the bus company got, the railway kept running, aided perhaps by the late evening trains added to the timetable at the end of the War, to remain ever afterwards.

Following the War the 'shop grey' paint used on the locomotives continued, although, as a small compensation, the coupling rods sometimes kept their red paint. Langley Aldrich assumes that the re-grouping of the railways was to come about in 1923 and it hardly seemed worthwhile to paint them twice. One or two were able to escape this treatment, however. The G.E.R. blue paint was of such good quality that it showed through the grey, producing some very off-putting colours. Because of this, some had to be repainted and the line's regular loco, No. 1121, was one of these.

In 1919 the carriages were painted crimson, a pleasant change from the previous dull brown and, by 1920, the *Crystal Palace* engines had returned.

For the enthusiast, the locomotives *not* allowed to run on the line at that time were, and I use the L.N.E.R. references: T19, *Humpty Dumpty,* N7, J16-19, D15/16, *Claud* and B12.

There was now no need for the porter to risk his neck lighting the carriage lamps as they were no longer open flame, but incandescent gas mantles.

In 1922 Brightlingsea Signal Box was removed, as it was no longer necessary, and the points were moved, as from 30th

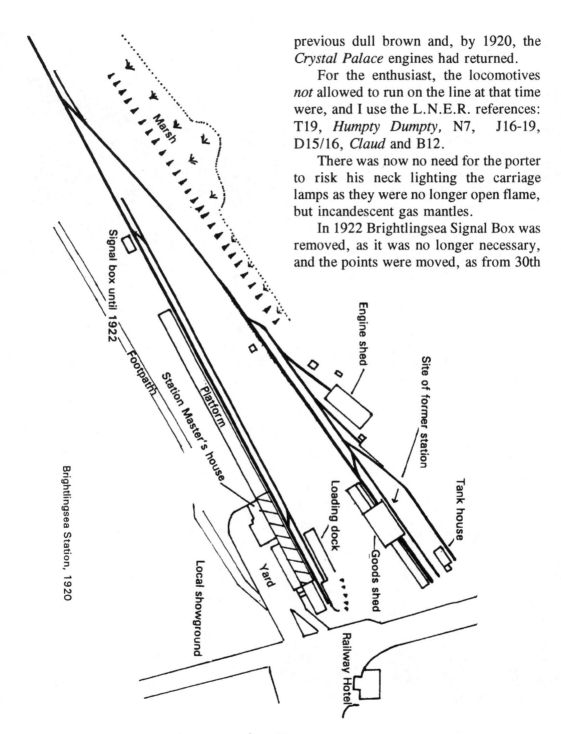

Brightlingsea Station, 1920

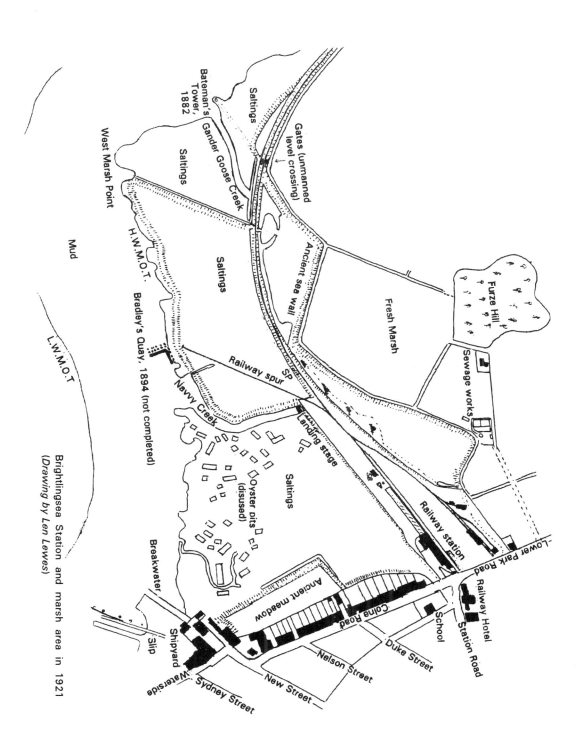

Bateman's Tower, 1882

West Marsh Point

Saltings

Gander Goose Creek

Saltings

Saltings

Mud

H.W.M.O.T.

Bradley's Quay, 1894 (not completed)

Navy Creek

L.W.M.O.T

Gates (unmanned level crossing)

Ancient sea wall

Fresh Marsh

Furze Hill

Sewage works

SP

Railway spur

Landing stage

Saltings

Oyster pits (disused)

Railway station

Lower Park Road

Railway Hotel

Station Road

School

Duke Street

Colne Road

Ancient meadow

Nelson Street

New Street

Breakwater

Shipyard

Slip

Waterside

Sydney Street

Brightlingsea Station and marsh area in 1921
(*Drawing by Len Lewes*)

89

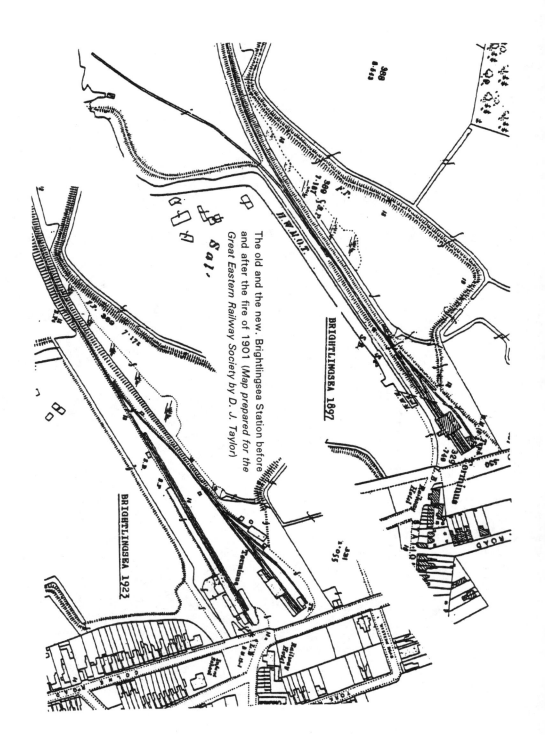

The old and the new. Brightlingsea Station before and after the fire of 1901 (*Map prepared for the Great Eastern Railway Society by D. J. Taylor*)

BRIGHTLINGSEA 1897

BRIGHTLINGSEA 1923

October, by means of three hand pulled levers situated on the ground beside the points themselves and another one frame lever in the Goods' Shed.

In the summer of 1922, in preparation for the grouping and the re-painting that was to follow, cleaners seemed not to care any more about the locomotives that once gleamed so proudly and they were allowed to get very dirty and neglected. In October, though, the clean up campaign was started again in preparation for the hand-over at the end of the year, but the only sponge cloths available for cleaning quickly turned the grey paint into a dirty khaki shade. In the re-shuffle of the previous year the yellow tender side G.E.R. had gone missing and large yellow numbers, similar to the system used in the Midland Railway, showed the locomotive number.

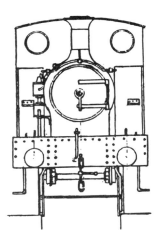

A visitor from the Colne Valley & Halstead Railway
The locomotive that helped up out in the mid 1920s

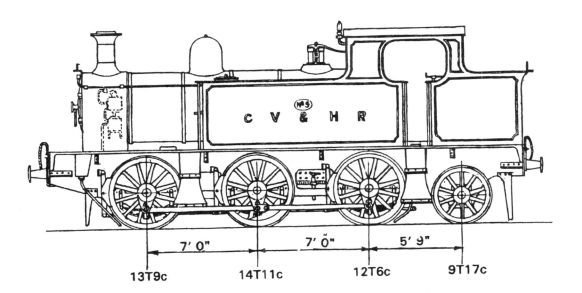

7' 0"   7' 0"   5' 9"

13T9c   14T11c   12T6c   9T17c

91

L.N.E.R.

At midnight on 31st December, 1922, the Great Eastern Railway ceased to be when it became part of the London & North Eastern Railway (L.N.E.R.), handing across 1,336 locomotives. Thus ended the Company that had been there at the Line's birth, always commanding, over-shadowing, and finally obtaining the Line - and now it was gone. As a small compensation, the numbers the loco-motives remained the same, or almost the same. The L.N.E.R. added 7,000 to each to be able to tell the difference between the various locomotives it had acquired from an assortment of companies, including some that had remained fiercely independent. The Colne Valley and Halstead, which it will be remembered were part of the Company building the line from Colchester North to Colchester Hythe, was absorbed into the L.N.E.R. after 67 years' independence.

Again, with the new Company, came the promised new colour scheme for the rolling stock. The battleship grey went forever, to be replaced by a glossy black outlined in red and the coaching stock changed to a teak livery, the former colour of Great Eastern stock. One hopes that the carriages had enjoyed their five years of crimson splendour. The smart green one associates with the romance and speed of these years of steam engines was kept for the larger tender passenger engines rarely seen on the line.

Another change that was to come about with the grouping was that, in addition to the usual white disc head codes the Brightlingsea branch usually carried showing the type of train (passenger, goods, etc.), a sign of a red disc with a white rim was added to the front of the train to indicate single line working. At night this was replaced by a red light and now, with a red light shining from both front and rear of the train, it needs little imagination to realise the trouble this caused. The L.N.E.R quickly abandoned the practice.

In 1925 a newcomer arrived on the line. This was rather special, as it had been part of the old Colne Valley and Halstead Railway. It was an old 0-6-2T locomotive built by Hudswell Clarke in 1908. It had started life as simply 'Number 5', but when acquired by the L.N.E.R. in March, 1924, became 8314 of Class N 18. In its early C.V. & H.R. days it was black with red lining and so was probably left alone when the change-over came. It was not to last long, being scrapped in 1928.

The *Crystal Palaces* were finally to leave in 1925, when they were replaced by a heavier class of engine, the 8040 Series Class F3. These 2-4-2Ts were to remain on the line until the start of World War II. Many *Crystal Palaces* were to have a short life, in some cases only 30 years. 1300, the local one, was

Platelayer George Studd poses in front of 8074 (Class F3) locomotive at Brightlingsea in June, 1930

built 1909 and scrapped in 1938. Strange to see such an early death for these locomotives, as other classes often had working lives of 80 years or more.

Now, once again, came attacks on the line's existence that were to be a part of its history. It can be doubted if many lines suffered so much attack from financial advisers or the sea and survived so long. The new owners, the L.N.E.R., were worried about the Swing Bridge. It was an additional cost, they argued, and had to be opened at unusual hours, as it depended on the tides, to allow shipping to pass to the Tidal Mill or sand workings. It was pointed out that with passenger and goods traffic combined the line was making £30,000 year for them, so it was decided the line should remain

and mechanisation of the bridge locking equipment, one of their points for closure, went ahead. By 1932 it could be locked or unlocked, if in possession of train staff, from either end of the line by means of electricity.

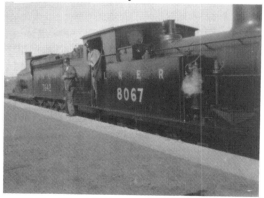

8067 Class F3 and 7642 Class J15 at Brightlingsea in the 1930's (*Photo C. Langley Aldrich*)

A train passes over the Swing Bridge in the early 1950's (*Photo courtesy of Peter Fisher*)

A train passes over the Swing Bridge in the early 1950's (*Photo courtesy of Peter Fisher*)

Only the bridge locks could be controlled and there were no plans to swing the bridge automatically, this still having to be done by hand using the T bar. But the days of the Pilotman and his cottage were drawing to a close. Shipping in Alresford Creek had begun to decline and a few years later it was sufficient for a porter to walk from Wivenhoe Station for the occasions that the bridge needed to be opened.

The installation of telephones at the same time helped to bring about an interesting piece of signalling. If an unscheduled train was to travel on the line, the train before it would carry a red board on the rear coach near the tail lamp. It measured 2 feet by 1½ feet, with the corners cut off.

The so-called 'Annett's Key' operating the bridge locking mechanism was, as has been said, situated on the staff itself and so, without going into a lengthy description, it will be realised that, if the key has to be inserted in the apparatus located at the stations in order to open the bridge locks, and if any train travelling on the line has to be in possession of the staff, it will be understood that it would have been impossible to open the bridge while there was a train on the track.

Before the Pilotman was made obsolete, with the coming of the 8 hour day in 1919, helped by the formation of the N.U.R. six years before, it not only meant that the Pilotman still had the Bridge to open prior to the electrification, but also that he had to have an assistant. Such a situation can bring about a happy ending. The Bridge Pilot at this time was Steve Bullard, who lived with his wife and daughter in the bridge cottage. He was helped in his work by Rupert Watsham, who came from Alresford each day to help him with alternate early and

94

About to cross the Swing Bridge from the Brightlingsea side behind Class J15 65432 on 7th July, 1956. The pilotman's cottage can be seen on the other side of the bridge (*Photo H. C. Casserley*)

late shifts. Rupert and Lillian, Mr Bullard's daughter, inevitably saw a lot of each other and eventually Rupert became the crossing keeper at Alresford Station with Lillian as his wife.

As well as the porter from Wivenhoe opening the Bridge, a platelayer would do the same job and the procedure was as follows: a 'phone call from Alresford Sand & Ballast Company would tell Wivenhoe Station that a barge was coming on the next tide. The porter or platelayer would walk to the bridge, remove the fishplate from the rails, ensuring that the locks were opened, and wait until the barge appeared before opening the bridge itself .

Before the coming of the 8 hour day, the work had been arduous and long. Mr

Wheeler, when starting in 1917, worked a 12 hour day with 3 days' holiday a year and a pass for railway travel within the G.E.R. territory. The rules were as follows: You were not allowed to do more than 14 hours without special permission in one day, more than 6 hours without a meal break, and had to have 8 hours rest before starting another shift.

The working conditions of the men looking after the horses at Wivenhoe before 1919 with less than five years' service to the railway company are worth considering. Normal working time was 13 hours a day with time off for meals. As they were allowed one Bank Holiday off in three, this, added to their annual holiday of three days, made a total of four days' holiday a year in all. There was no overtime paid for working on Sundays. In case of time off due to accident or illness, a penny a week could be paid into a fund to ensure that you had at least some money coming in over any period you might be off work.

The arrangement for stopping trains at White House Beach was to continue after the Great War and it remained a stopping place for swimmers or pic-nickers until the 1940s. Stopping the train did not even have to be arranged, for in the summer months the engine crews were always on the lookout for a wave from a carriage window or the lineside as they passed the spot. There was a warmth about the railway in the inter-war years that did not only come from the fire-box!

The Pilotman's cottage was to continue to be lived in until the 1950s, but no longer by men of the railway. A local farmer used to let a worker, with the appropriate name of Samson, use it for himself and his family. The interest in the cottage for schoolboys using the line was that the garden had an apple tree growing close to the line. It was not difficult to grab at an apple as the train went by slowly after its journey across the Bridge. However, a sharp cut across the back of the hand by an apple branch temporarily cooled the desire for a free apple that was a cooker anyway. The practice finally stopped when one boy got his hand jammed in a branch and nearly got pulled out of the carriage window, being held back in the nick of time by his friends when his feet left the compartment floor.

A view of the usual three carriages, the first is part guard's van. It is one of the draughty clerestory type that the guards disliked so much that they tried to 'lose' it. (*Photo Philip Conolly*)

The cottage had a telephone used to tell the station staff when the Bridge was opened or closed and this telephone came in very handy for another schoolboy prank. One winter's evening before the Second World War the schoolchildren stocked up with a good supply of snowballs and, as the train slowed down for the Bridge, pelted the Bridge Pilot. When the train arrived at Brightlingsea the staff came along locking the doors and nobody was allowed out until the culprits owned up.

Now that the line was again reprieved, steam heating was introduced to the coaches in 1926. Once the strange hiss from under the seat had been identified, passengers much appreciated the warmth and comfort, though this comfort was sometimes marred by sprats being carefully placed on the heaters by schoolboys.

By the mid 30s the six wheeled coaches disappeared and were replaced by bogie stock, although this was often very much second hand from other pre-L.N.E.R. Companies. "Rather a shame," comments Dr Ian Allen, "Whereas the bogie coaches gave familiar side to side motion, that of the six wheelers was more of a forward and backward motion, much more preferable."

From about 1938 three-coach sets usually ran on the line. These usually comprised a brake third, a first and a third class composite (mixed), and a third class carriage. As was the case on many of the old Great Eastern branches, these were an odd assortment of G.E.R., N.E.R., and early L.N.E.R. stock, and a right mix up they sometimes were. Some would have looked more at home in an historical film of Victorian or Edwardian days, with carved wood panelling and ancient highly sprung green seats.

Instead of using special goods trains, one or two goods wagons were often attached to many of the passenger trains. The freight was varied, but perhaps the strangest cargo the line ever carried was two elephants brought down by a visiting circus. The shipyards ensured a varied freight too, the most important being the valuable 'native' oyster.

The largest cargo.
A motor launch over 40ft long and 9ft wide prepares to leave Brightlingsea for Swansea on 6th May, 1934.
(*Photo courtesy Miss B. Foster*)

Leaving the Swing Bridge on the Brightlingsea side, the wooded area to the left is Noah's Ark. July 7th, 1956, travelling on the 4.21 p.m. from St Botolph's, Colchester (*Photo H. C. Casserley*)

SHIPPED BY TRAIN

The Romans it was who first found Colne oysters palatable. From Colchester the Romans came to Brightlingsea by means of a ford across Alresford Creek. In Noah's Ark a Roman villa stood in an area close to the sea. Other extensive Roman remains were found in a villa site in 1884, close to the Alresford side of the Swing Bridge. Excavations in the Noah's Ark area have revealed piles of oyster shells left by the Roman settlers. These piles would be searched through by children in the hope of finding Roman coins, but never with success.

Not all the oysters dealt with in Brightlingsea were 'Colchester Natives', which got their name from Colchester having claim to the river. Arthur Cox, a porter on Brightlingsea Station explains,

"Oysters were mostly imported from Portugal, arriving here in trucks as seedlings about March or April. These were laid on Brightlingsea oyster beds to grow, and later became large Portuguese oysters which were the main dispatch during the summer months to various resorts for sale at shellfish stalls at the seaside towns of Blackpool, Scarborough, Southend and many other places."

Colchester Native oysters were dispatched from September until March - when there was an 'R' in the month - mainly to London markets and hotels. Other consignments went in small quantities to individual customers. There used to be wicker baskets of oysters, covered in sacking, on the station platform ready for loading into the

Guard's van or one or two wagons attached to passenger trains. As a reward for loading the oysters, the station staff went home at the end of each week with 25 given to them in a small sacking bag.

There was one freight, the freight that built the line, that for quantity even outdid the oyster.

A young girl, the grand-daughter of the owners of the Anchor Hotel at Brightlingsea, would wait by the telephone about October or November time. When the long-awaited message came, she would run to the Hard shouting, "The sprats are in at Aldeburgh." The sprats had begun their journey from the Arctic and now money would come into the town again, as everybody had been living on credit until then, and foreign coins had become an accepted sight in the till.

The Anchor served the sprat men well. It never kept to licensing hours during the spratting season and one could imagine the gratitude of the men coming to the Hard at 5 on a cold November morning and being able to obtain hot coffee with plenty of rum in it, as Mr Percival, the landlord, used to set up a table on the Hard in the cold winter weather and serve either coffee with rum and milk or milk and rum.

The 'Stowboaters' would go out time and time again when the sprats arrived at Brightlingsea on their journey southward. They were caught by letting down nets from anchored boats and, as the tide flowed, the sprats were driven backward by the force of the current into them. Looking for seabirds was a sure way of locating the fish. On good days the nets would look like large sausages with the weight of the catches. A rowing boat even ran aground on one of the nets, so tightly packed were the fish.

The sprats would be taken to the

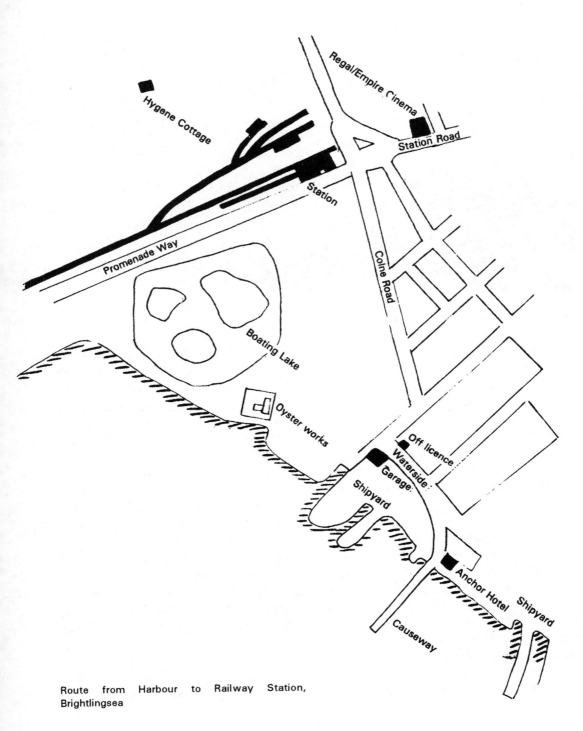

Route from Harbour to Railway Station, Brightlingsea

n via Colne Road by either horse cart or handcart, and a small rm had been built, so that they be unloaded from the road. Before : Road was built in 1888, orchards ed the land and the route from the ur to the Station was difficult, as it ed going up New Street, through ria Place and down Station Road. In 920s the road was unsurfaced and f mud with salt water upon it. After trips the carts would sink in to axles. To help relieve unemploy- in the 1930s, the Council decided to concrete surface on the road as an iment, so that the dropped fish be easily swept away. The road :o be so full of fallen fish during the ing season that the children called it r Street'. Train passengers had to

splash through sprats to get to the station. From November to February trains often carried up to 20 ferry wagons, the record being 21 going from Harwich to Belgium in January, 1937. Those leaving Bright-lingsea at 1.15 p.m. arrived at Zeebrugge at 7 a.m. the next day and were on sale shortly afterwards. These trains left three or four days a week, carrying the sprats that had been purchased by Belgian merchants, who would come across to buy the sprats to be taken to Parkeston Quay for shipping to the continent.

The price in December, when the sprats were full of oil, was about 2p for a bushel (56 lb) in the 1930s, now they sell at over 80p per pound! The unwanted fish at Wivenhoe were always left in a big gleaming heap on the quay for locals to come with buckets and help them-

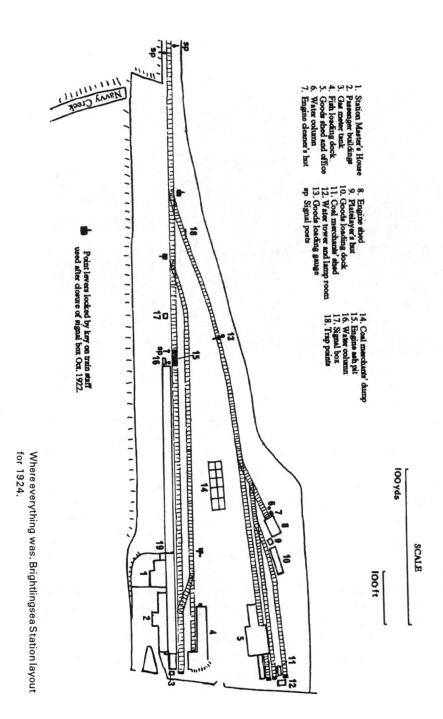

SCALE

100 yds

100 ft

1. Station Master's House
2. Passenger buildings
3. Gas meter tank
4. Fish loading dock
5. Goods shed and office
6. Water column
7. Engine cleaner's hut

8. Engine shed
9. Platelayer's hut
10. Goods loading dock
11. Coal merchants' shed
12. Water tower and lamp room
13. Goods loading gauge
sp Signal posts

14. Coal merchants' dump
15. Engine ash pit
16. Water column
17. Signal box
18. Trap points

Point levers locked by key on train staff
used after closure of signal box Oct. 1922.

Navvy Creek

Where everything was. Brightlingsea Station layout
for 1924.

Sprats smoked in Brightlingsea in the yard behind Victoria Place.

selves. Others would be sent away by boat for use as fish manure.

Like all harvests of the sea, it depended on several factors to determine how many fish were caught. One year, in contrast to the money that was usually gained, one fisherman was £5 out of pocket.

One Brightlingsea character hit on a simple way of making money. He would take orders, go down to the station, remove the labels from boxes and replace them with his own. It is reported by those who know about such things that he never bought a sprat in his life.

Some sprats were pickled or smoked at Brightlingsea before their journey. A train of 13 trucks would take them away and, as one railway porter commented, "They looked like silver."

Many sprats went no further than the Hythe - to Edgars' Canning Factory. It was said that you could always tell girls from Edgars even for a long time after they had stopped being employed there! One man would come home to his mother on a Friday night and throw his wage packet on the table with always the same comment, "Do that stink?"

The sprats destined to go as manure were taken by boat, as has been said before, to Wivenhoe for loading on the railway. Hervey Benham in his book *The Stowboaters* tells of how the sprat boat men would have to caulk the sides of the railway truck with mud to keep the water in; it all added to the weight, and that was how they were paid. Just to make sure they made their money, they would try to fool the man operating the weigh-bridge by all going round to the blind side of the truck and swinging on it while it was being weighed.

It was partly for the sprats that the

railway had been founded and they were a profitable business, a special train running to Manningtree every Sunday during the 'season' to aid carriage abroad. Fish was also sent to Scotland for curing. The total time for the journey to Dundee was 22 hours, the trucks travelling by way of Ipswich, Ely and March, where they would join the Great Eastern and Great Northern Joint Line and from Doncaster would head north on the North Eastern Railway. A ride on that train would have been quite an experience.

Shrimps were yet another sea cargo that went by rail from Brightlingsea. The Tollesbury men, known as the 'Tolly-boys' would come to Brightlingsea in the evenings and, after the development of the West Marsh when Navvy Creek was no longer used, would leave their oil drums for fuel at a garage on the way from the Station to the Hard and, coming back, those oil drums, now filled, would be picked up and taken aboard. They would stay in the Creek for the night, going off early the next morning for another day's shrimping.

These were busy times, even in relation to other occupations, for railway workers at that time.

Between the Wars, with increased train services, two locomotives were needed to work the branch. One of these engines would be kept at Brightlingsea overnight, the cleaner travelling down on the last train and then would spend the night, from midnight until 8 the following morning, cleaning and over-hauling the engine for its next day's

work. This all sounds simple, but at Brightlingsea this is a full explanation of what he had to do:

First, he had to unload the coal from the standing wagons and bring it to the staging near the locomotive; when the engine had cooled down he had to clean out the firebox and then fill the engine with coal; next, came an examination of the engine, even down to looking at the underside; finally, the engine had to be steamed up for the first morning run at 6. For this work he was paid £2.10s. From the 1920s he had a companion for part of the night, who cleaned the carriages. All this was to cease when the engines became shedded at Colchester.

The day of the driver and the fireman began with the 6 a.m. train running to Wivenhoe to connect with the first train from Clacton to Colchester. The after-noon staff came on duty at 2.30 to relieve them and they continued until the last train at 10 p.m.

When the trains were absent there was always work for the station staff, which could include the mixing up of various chemical formulæ like the white-wash used to mark the edge of the platform. This line was to be no more than 5 inches in width and the formula was made up of 4 lb whitening, 1 pint of stiff size, 4 pint of boiled oil and 3 pint of boiled turps, "sufficient water to be added to bring the mixture to the consistency of cream." Mixtures could also be made up for the cleaning of rolling stock used by horses, asses or mules, including 'the sides of the vehicle and all other parts thereof with which the

Wivenhoe Junction after the signal box had gone. A goods train from Brightlingsea is about to join the main line. 1948 (*Photo G. H. Lake*)

head or any discharge from the mouth or nostrils has come into contact." The mixture for this: pour 2 gallons of water into a pail, add 1 lb of good dry chloride of lime and stir well with a wooden stick. These recipes have been taken from the G.E.R. instructions of 1919.

These instructions were sometimes very severe, as with the concern for fire hazards. If a train were 'mixed' - both carriages and freight - and one wagon due to be part of the train contained amongst its general goods one case of matches, it would then have to be labelled 'Inflammable goods' and be left off the train at Wivenhoe, until an engine and brake van could return for it, usually in the evening when there was a gap in the working timetable.

No shunting was allowed to be carried out at Brightlingsea unless the branch engine was there, and, if shunting with a train or vehicles had to be done at Wivenhoe Junction involving using the branch, if the engine was not present a man with hand signals and detonators had to be sent 1,000 yards down the line beyond the home signal. In fog or falling snow, two detonators had to be placed on the line 200 yards in advance of the Junction Box.

Promotion for the railwaymen was slow and done strictly on the basis of the number of years worked for the Company. If nine people were higher than you on the promotion list, then it was a matter of waiting until those nine had, in their turn, been promoted. The

L.N.E.R. would distribute a notice stating the date when the newest promoted man had joined the Company. If a railwayman had joined before that date, he was to apply to the Company and be given his promotion. The order of promotion was Cleaner; Passed Cleaner (having passed his promotion exams); Fireman; Acting Driver; and then Driver. The Passed Cleaner did the job of the Fireman during staff holidays or at any other time he was needed.

There were now 11 trains each way on weekdays and, in 1936, the Summer Service seemed so popular that it was decided to give it a try during the winter months to see if this popularity continued. It was so successful after its trial run that it stayed. A surprising thing was that, by 1947, the branch had seven trains each way during the winter on Sundays - more than the Clacton and Walton line.

The last train left Brightlingsea at 8.57 p.m., but returned at 9.52 for its overnight stay. There was now a 9.58 p.m. on Saturdays only and, if anybody had the stamina or the absolute determination to get to London, they could go as far as Liverpool Street on that train and the help of various connections and arrive at 3.40 a.m. The third class monthly return now cost 11/- (55p) to London, but on that last train it would have perhaps been more sporting if they had paid you!

The population of Brightlingsea was now 4,145. It was to be only 4,500 at the closure of the line - and to think that it had once been so close to becoming another Yarmouth or Lowestoft!

Between 1918 and 1939 the type of passenger carried on the line changed in keeping with the change in the yachting world. The owners of the large steam yachts anchored in the Creek at Brightlingsea gave up their pastime. These yachts used to have a crew of between 22 and 26 on the larger vessels and such craft as the *Rosabelle* and the *Lorna* were names well known in Brightlingsea. They finally disappeared during World War II, when they were taken for use by Coastal patrol and other naval duties.

The mention of steam yachts always brings a flood of amusing stories about the eccentric American millionaire, Bayard Brown, who will already be remembered as the generous helper of the poor during the bad sprat harvests of the

Bayard Brown, eccentric and benefactor of Brightlingsea. He usually moved in group photographs to make sure his photograph wasn't taken, but this is a posed portrait.

1880s. His behaviour became ever more peculiar in later years and he did not, as many other steam yacht owners did, leave Brightlingsea Creek with the end of the steam yacht era, although his craft *Valfreya* was first anchored in Brightlingsea Creek in June, 1889. The vessel was always steamed up ready to go to sea, but never went anywhere and Bayard Brown was to remain in Brightlingsea or Wivenhoe until his death during the Second World War.

He would occasionally travel to London from Brightlingsea, being driven to the station in a horse and cart, when he would loudly grunt for attention. Mr Wheeler tells of being a young porter when Bayard Brown went by train. He entered the station, bought a first class ticket with a five pound note and told the ticket clerk to keep the change. Then he went about giving out ten shilling notes to the station staff and an undisclosed sum to the Station Master. Mr Wheeler had been told to take his case to ensure a good tip, and then stand beside the compartment door when arrived. When Bayard Brown finally got into his compartment, he reached into his back pocket, and muttering, "I don't like the look of you!" he handed across three ha'pence. Apparently if he liked a person then that person was sure of money; if he didn't, and there was no reason for his dislikes, then there was little chance of receiving his generosity.

He used to throw gold sovereigns from his yacht to people in boats that would crowd alongside, especially when the news got around Brightlingsea that he

was in a 'giving' mood. Then he would just as soon shout to the boatmen to go away, as he didn't like them. Sometimes he would throw the sovereigns into the water on purpose, just to watch the anger on the faces of the boatmen as a week's wages sank into the sea.

Once though, his cunning was matched. Another of his jokes was to heat up sovereigns in a frying pan held over a fire. He would then drop them over the side where they would be eagerly grabbed by the waiting crowd, only to be let go of very quickly to sink into the water. After one such episode, the thrifty men of Brightlingsea went away - to return wearing gloves.

Two ladies came to Brightlingsea from Wivenhoe to go aboard his yacht once a week. They were reputed to have been far from attractive, but always came ashore with enough money to stop at Mr Went's off-licence for a bottle of gin. This would be drunk while they sat in the Waiting Room until the train arrived and they often had to be carried into their compartments by the station staff for their journey home. The staff would then 'phone ahead to Wivenhoe to let them know they were coming.

Despite his eccentricities, however, Bayard Brown gave a Recreation ground and almshouses for the town and, in return, Brightlingsea named an Avenue in his honour. It is estimated that he gave away a quarter of a million pounds whilst his boat was in the Creek.

After 29 years of being pestered in Brightlingsea, he moved to Wivenhoe, mooring his boat in the Creek. Here he would appear suddenly in the station entrance wearing a double-breasted reefer jacket and cheesecutter hat, which were his normal clothes - he did not always bother to wear any while on board. After buying his first-class ticket with the same amount of show that he had used in Brightlingsea, he would go off to London - to get a haircut.

The railway's last tribute was to take his body, following his death on his yacht at Wivenhoe, to London. He was eventually buried in America.

The reason for the slow decline of the steam yachts was that some of the owners had been killed in the Great War. Added to this, taxation of income meant that it was not so easy to keep a yacht maintained and crewed for the occasional weekend use. The pleasure seekers turned to the new attractions of the motor car and so evolved the ordinary man with the small yacht or boat that he sailed himself. This led to the popularity of the Colne Yacht Club and the Brightlingsea and Wivenhoe Sailing Clubs. Although the Brightlingsea Sailing Club was founded in 1885, it really got under way in 1921 after a few years of success or failure. The Colne Yacht Club at Brightlingsea was founded in 1919, although it had existed in various forms at Wivenhoe since before 1873.

All this meant more people coming to Brightlingsea in the summer and the idea of holidays by the sea for the working man and his family was to change the face of Brightlingsea's West Marsh, running alongside the railway for its first half-mile and containing the remains of

Bateman's Tower in 1906. Built by Squire Bateman so that boats could find their way home. (*Author's collection*)

Bradley's Quay and Navvy Creek.

To offer employment during the depression years of the early 30s a scheme was planned to build up the Marsh as a pleasure area. St Botolph's sidings were being excavated at Colchester and so the soil was brought to Brightlingsea. A perfect situation, as the track ran alongside the site. Navvy Creek was filled in, with the exception of its mouth, which was to become the base of the new swimming pool.

The railway had open marsh on both sides, as can be seen in early photographs, the main attraction of them being, until then, for both railwaymen and young boys, large anthills, some almost 3 feet high, which could be, and often were, kicked over for the delight of seeing startled ants running in all

108

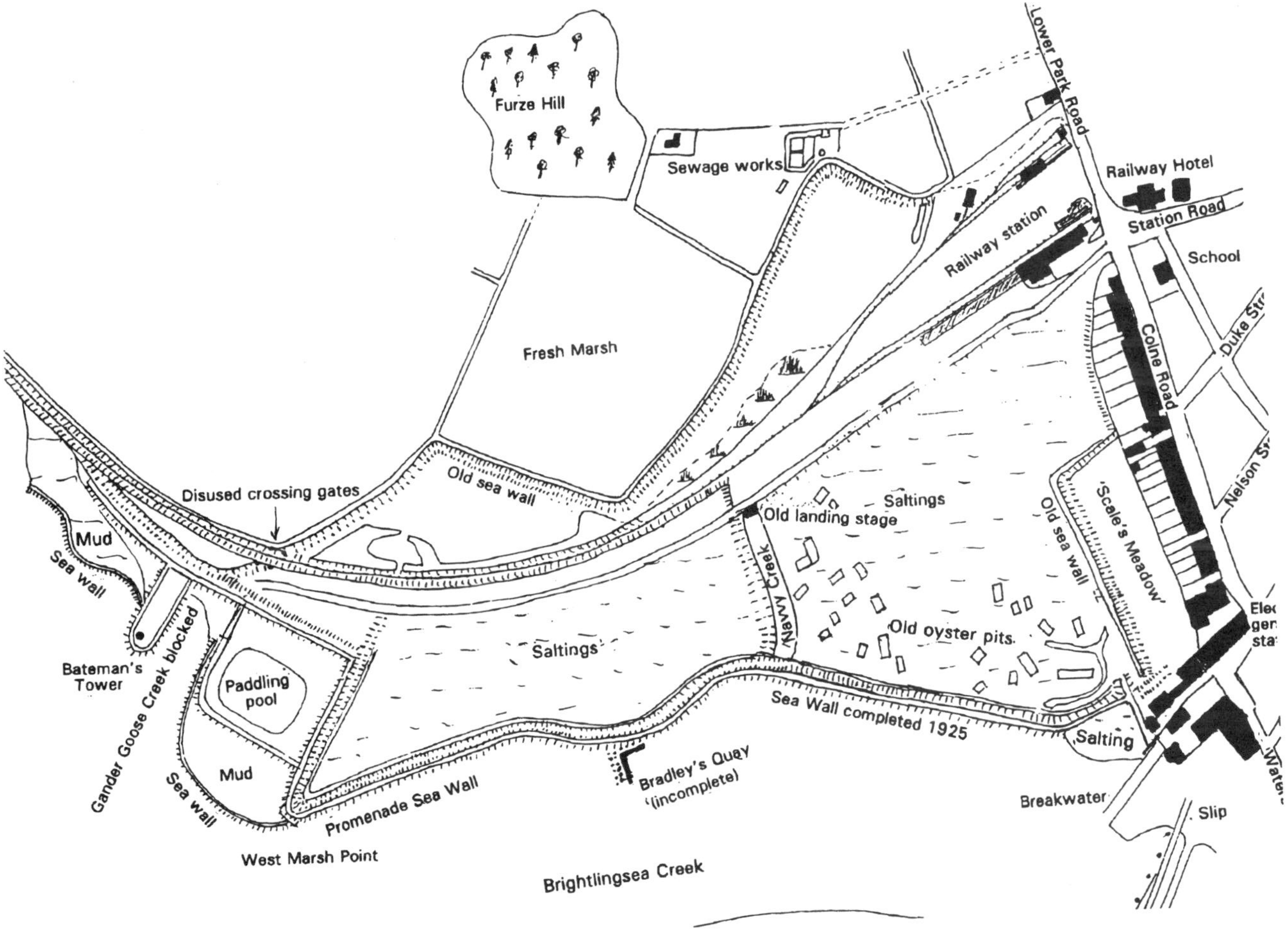

Two contrasting maps; before and after the building of the Brightlingsea holiday area in the early 1930s (*Maps by Len Lewes*)

Brightlingsea Creek

Labels on map:

Sea wall
Mud
Bateman's Tower
Gander Goose Creek 'blocked'
Sea wall
Mud
West Marsh Point
Paddling pool
Promenade Sea Wall
Disused crossing gates
Old sea wall
Fresh Marsh
Furze Hill
Saltings
Bradley's Quay '(incomplete)'
Sewage works
'Navvy Creek'
Old landing stage
Saltings
Sea Wall completed 1925
Old oyster pits
Railway station
Lower Park Road
Breakwater
Salting
Old sea wall
'Scale's Meadow'
Railway Hotel
Station Road
Colne Road
School
Slip
Nelson St.
Duke Str.
Eler ger sta
Water

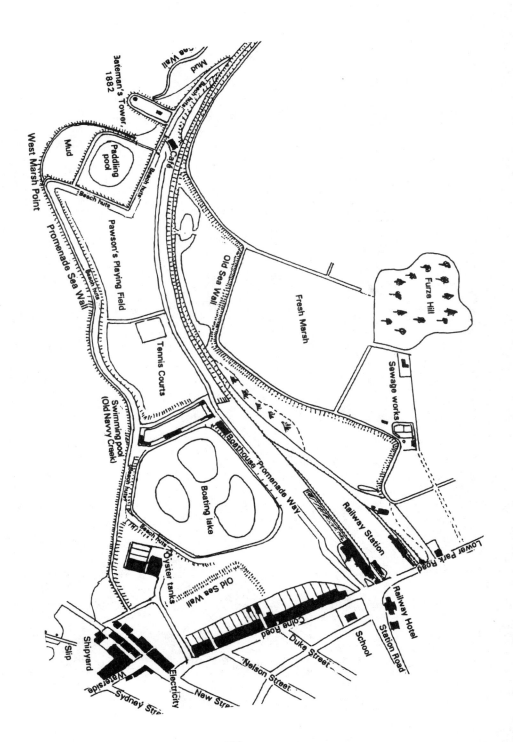

Sea Wall

Mud

Bateman's Tower, 1882

Beach huts

Mud

West Marsh Point

Paddling pool

Café

Beach huts

Promenade Sea Wall

Pawson's Playing Field

Beach huts

Old Sea Wall

Fresh Marsh

Furze Hill

Tennis Courts

Sewage works

Swimming pool (Old Navvy Creek)

Beach huts

Boathouse

Promenade Way

Boating lake

Railway Station

Beach huts

Oyster tanks

Lower Park Road

Old Sea Wall

Colne Road

Railway Hotel

Slip

Shipyard

Duke Street

School

Station Road

Waterside

Electricity

Nelson Street

Sydney Street

New Street

110

directions. Bateman's Tower, standing on a bank of mud that had to be climbed up to reach the base, was now to be placed on a more solid piece of land.

Councillors had lent money for the project, which cost £28,000, with £7,000 spent on labour, for which the Government provided 90% of the money. 185 men were given jobs, which, at a time when any job was difficult to find and money seemed unobtainable by any honest means, must have seemed a miracle. They were paid ninepence a day and were expected to bring their own boots and waterproofs. The wage was by no means guaranteed as in very wet weather there was no work and this meant no pay. Their main task was the building of a boating lake using wooden barrows to shift the spoil.

Part of the project was by no means new: a parish magazine for 1911 submitted that the West Marsh should be purchased and laid out as a park to commemorate the Coronation of George V. After the First World War a contract was signed for the erection of a sea wall, but although promises had been made, no work was done. However, the land had been bought by the Council for £900 in May, 1918, half coming from the District Fund and half from interest-free loans from townspeople.

With the opening of the West Marsh Pleasure Grounds and the eightpenny return to Colchester, passenger traffic rose considerably. This was just what was needed, for, as R S Joby says, the advent of the motor car and good roads meant the decline of many lines between 1927 and 1931.

On 23rd June, 1932, when the West Marsh was officially opened by the Mayor of Colchester, Councillor Hazell, no fewer than 5,000 trippers arrived and it was not unusual after that to have 3,000 visitors on Thursdays (as this was early closing day in Colchester and shop assistants, as well as the general public, would come to Brightlingsea for an afternoon by the sea). The weather had a great influence on the number of passengers, but, given a fine Sunday and a high tide, one could expect 3,000 passengers to arrive at a town with only 4,000 population.

The day of the West Marsh opening is best remembered by the Brightlingsea people because of the weather. Although the *Brightlingsea Times* wrote of it as a day when "glorious sunshine prevailed throughout Tuesday, and a huge crowd gathered on West Marsh for the ceremony", there was a sudden violent downpour and the bedraggled visitors gathered together on the station for shelter. Many say that it has never rained so hard since.

Pawson's Playground, named in memory of a local schoolmaster, was opened the following year.

The land to the left of the station was the accepted site for travelling shows since the opening of the railway. George Bradley had been called all the way to Colchester to give evidence about right of public access to West Marsh and quoted the fact, thereby stopping the plans of one of the new Manor Lords for using it for another purpose.

The local 'showground' stands to the left of the station. Home for visiting fairs, circuses and all travelling showmen. (*Postcard*)

Harry Carr and his Merry Scamps. The pierrot show for Brightlingsea, which performed near the station in 1912. (*Photo courtesy of Clive Vinson*)

In 1912 a pierrot show, 'Harry Carr and his Merry Scamps', performed during the summer months in a fenced off area close to the station, called in the advertisements 'Cosycorner', on a stage surrounded by sacking on poles. When the show opened in June tickets were 1/-, 6d and 3d: by July the prices had fallen to 6d, 4d and 2d and customers were advised to 'look out for Sacred Concerts'. By August things were so bad that there was even a 'Harry Carr's Benefit Night', before the show finally closed. The show at one stage boasted a live donkey, often followed by the next act - a man with a shovel. It must have had its attractions, however, for one old sailor still recalls, 70 years later, a chorus girl called Kitty Delaney, who used to perform with the troupe.

Close to the station on Boxing Day, 1912, stands the new Empire Cinema started by Harry Carr when his pierrot show failed in the summer of the same year (*Photo courtesy of Clive Vinson*)

Station Road, Brightlingsea, showing the railway buildings and, on the right, the new picture palace.

In 1912 the Empire Cinema, later called the Regal, opened at the bottom of Station Road, and Mr Carr, perhaps able to foresee the attractions of the bioscope, went into partnership with two others to become its first manager. The cinema was constructed at a cost of £50.

Entertainments now moved closer to the Waterside and the area was not used after that, Mack's Amusements opening at the Waterside site in the 1930s.

Passengers for Point Clear or the Stone also came to Brightlingsea by train and then had to be ferried from the Hard across the Creek by boatmen. There were often between 20 and 30 of these ferryboats to be hired before the War as the local authority did not feel the need for licences to limit numbers. A special race would be held in the annual Brightlingsea Regatta to test the ferrymen's speed and skill.

At first, these boatmen would wait on the Hard for their passengers, but it wasn't long before they started walking

How many people can you count? The Rowhedge ferry in about 1934, before regulations were tightened, carries part of a Sunday School outing.

Passengers for the railway used the ferry across from Point Clear, 1906. (*Author's collection*)

closer and closer to the station to attract customers. Eventually, they would even wait upon the station platform and the situation began to resemble that of the Far East as they fought for suitcases or possessions as security of them meant certain custom. A well-rehearsed line of patter would be, "I carried you last year, sir," "Mine's a good boat", and several others were amongst the usual phrases. The fare across to Point Clear was tuppence, but the board announcing this fact was difficult to find and the usual phrase was "I'll leave it to you, sir!"

Ballast was used, not only for the new West Marsh area, but also for the track itself. Eroded by frequent high tides, filling-in work was always needing to be done.

114

There were three bridges at that time, not including a small section of raised track, 263 feet in length, on the Wivenhoe side of the Wooden Bridge. The Swing Bridge has already been dealt with, then there was the Wooden Bridge, about one mile out of Brightlingsea Station, the remains of which could be seen until recently; now only the sawn-off stumps remain. Thirdly, there was another bridge between the two areas of marsh just past the Wooden Bridge, known as Long Bridge. The Wooden Bridge was 345 feet long and the Long Bridge 680 feet. This was filled in, as was the small section near the Wooden Bridge in about 1932: this had to be done each night with the aid of a 2 a.m. ballast train from Colchester. This was the only time it could be done without disrupting the train service. Railwaymen had to walk the five miles from Brightlingsea to Wivenhoe in order to hand the 'staff' to the signalman in the Junction Box, so the line could be opened. Sometimes, when the trains were sent from Colchester to do repair work at 5 a.m., Mr Wheeler used to get up at 2.45 a.m. to walk there by 4.45 and allow the train to pass.

This triangular brass staff was used on other lines to play a rather cruel trick on any signalman who had fallen out of favour with the train crews, remembers Driver Alan Wells. The staff was wrapped in a cloth and then held near the fire until it was nice and hot and then handed quickly to the waiting signalman - brass is good conductor of heat.

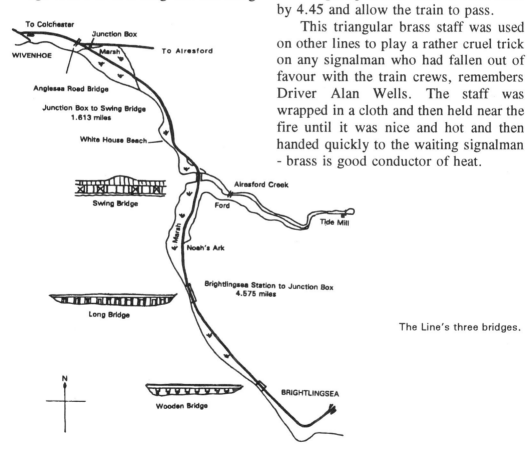

The Line's three bridges.

115

There was a quiet time during the busy period in the morning, when a train service to Cambridge started in 1921. This left Brightlingsea at 10.15 a m. and allowed a goods train to come in at midday. There was no return from Cambridge and the service ceased at the start of the Second World War.

Two accidents happened in the years between the Wars, one of which could have been serious. Arthur Nice, a Wivenhoe track walker, was doing his usual walk at 7.30 a.m. from Wivenhoe to Brightlingsea, when he noticed that the Swing Bridge centre span was 3 inches out of alignment. Unknown to him at the time, a sand barge, going up to the wharf at the start of Alresford Creek, had struck the side of the Bridge during the fog of the previous night. Realising that this could well cause a serious accident, for 3 inches alteration in a railway track is just as dangerous as several feet, Arthur ran back to the Pilotman's Cottage, where he was told that the train had just left Brightlingsea Station. He did the only thing possible and ran across the bridge to wave down the train before it reached the shifted rails. The local paper, reporting the event, spoke of his having run "50 yards before collapsing exhausted". After a week of waiting, during which Arthur must have been the subject of a few jokes from fellow workers, the paper printed a correction and an apology, "For 50 read 500".

Examination showed that although the bridge structure had shifted slightly, the foundation piles had not moved at all. Yet still the Brightlingsea people preferred the 'bus to Colchester rather than go by train for fear of the bridge collapsing. The mere fact that the train went over the bridge at 5 miles per hour proved they were sure, that there was 'summat wrong'.

Although this was supposed to be the first accident to occur concerning the bridge, in the 70 years of its history, perhaps it should be said 'notable' accident. The present owner of Moverons Farm, while lying awake as a boy, used to hear very angry conversations between the bargemen and the Bridge Pilot, as the barges bumped up against the bridge in the dark. Not only did it offer an interesting half hour or so for a young boy who was supposed to be asleep, but there was always the chance of learning new 'words'.

Once again, the friendly relationship existed between the men of the railway and the local landowners. Often the 'phone would ring and it would be someone at the Station reporting that their train driver or the guard had seen a bullock stuck in the mud or a sheep with its head stuck in a fence.

The other accident happened when an engine, shunting to connect with 25 fish wagons, came off the rails due to the points having been pulled too early. A crane had to be sent to Brightlingsea to hoist the engine back on the rails. This was one occasion when the 'staff ' proved to be a bit of a nuisance, as one of the Brightlingsea porters had to walk to the Junction Box, staff in hand, to enable the breakdown crane to get through. This, in fact, happened every

A steam crane lifts a derailed locomotive back on to the lines. 23rd August, 1935 (*Photo East Anglian Daily Times*)

time an engine failed, due to any reason, to make the return journey to Wivenhoe. The age of the motor car gradually phased out the walk.

Wivenhoe Junction Box was closed on 17th July, 1938, and the working transferred to the box at Wivenhoe Station, although, oddly, the Junction Box continued to be used for a while as a place where the railway workers met to pay their Union dues. The Brightlingsea line had now become, in fact, 'a branch off a branch'.

The Box might have been closed, but the memory of Bert Exworth, the friendly man at the Junction Box, who never received a 'heated staff', was to live on in the minds of Wivenhoe children, whom he befriended, for the rest of their lives. Quite illegally he would let them

into the box after they had scampered across the track. There they always got their first glimpse of the iron grey hair, the little white moustache and the peaked cap that he always wore, that was Bert. Local story has it that his hair went white soon after the Lily Wade incident, although he was only in his thirties.

He kept the Junction Box in spotless condition, even down to the pegged rug on the floor. The children were not only invited in to admire it, but to help keep it smart. Lamps had to be cleaned and the white paint of the box made to look even whiter with scrubbing. In winter he would make tea on the stove or heat up food that he had brought with him in his can. This can was Company Issue and is still recalled as being deep blue outside and white enamel inside. In this children

Ted Hills, the regular Brightlingsea guard, retires, 31st October, 1924. Many of the station staff, especially those on the left, were to stay with the line for the rest of its existence.
(*Photo Douglas Went*)

would collect food from his wife and walk carefully from Station Road, where he lived, down to the Box and give it to him. Bert had started as a Telegraph Boy at Witham station in 1887 and saw 39 years railway service at Wivenhoe station before the presentation of an umbrella by the Railway Company and his retirement in 1937. During this time he had seen seven Station Masters come and go at Wivenhoe. As with Brightlingsea, they never seemed to last long.

The other man who was remembered as working in the Junction Box was Bernard Dixie and it is sad to end the story of this signal box with another fatal accident, but that was the way it was.

In late April, Mark Foster took a Saturday evening stroll down Anglesea Road to discuss ambulance work with Bernard Dixie, who was the signalman on duty in the Box. Although a railway employee - he had just started as a ganger three weeks before - this was illegal by Railway Law, but it was a case of 'everybody did it' - remember Bert Exworth and the children. After his chat he walked back down the line towards Wivenhoe when a train passed him coming out of Wivenhoe towards Alresford. The noise of the train made him fail to hear another coming up behind him. The fireman shouted to the driver, who slammed the brakes on and sounded the whistle, but nothing could have stopped the train in that distance and the fireman shouted that he had seen a figure hit by the train as it went past. Foster's body was found later and Bernard Dixie was in tears at the Inquest the following Wednesday. Any talk that it was somebody's fault that Mark Foster was on the line at all was ignored.

The Brightlingsea train waits in Wivenhoe sidings for the London train to pass and go on to the station. Then it will shortly pick up passengers for Brightlingsea. Early 1940s (*Photo Philip Conolly*)

PRE-WAR

Wivenhoe Station during these pre-war years was to see many excursion trains from the Midlands and East Anglia *en route* to Clacton and the sea. A day out for the family might have cost a man a week's wages, but it was considered well worth it. These excursions often included very out-of-the-way places in their pick-up points. It is not easy to find Waplode or Counter Drove on a map, but many people in these areas still treasure memories of such trips.

The Brightlingsea poor, while not getting such excursions, could still benefit from the railway, when the Deputy Mayor's Christmas Fund annually provided them with a truck of coal for distribution amongst the needy.

At the start of the Second World War, the engines ceased to be shedded at Brightlingsea, returning each evening to Colchester. This caused hardship for any man working on the trains whose home was in Brightlingsea. Basil Watson, a driver, having made the last run to Brightlingsea and then taking the empty train back to Colchester, faced a cycle ride home each night and another back the following morning. This two way journey often totalled 115 miles a week.

Although coal for the locomotive ceased to be kept in bulk at Brightlingsea, a pile was kept during the remaining days of steam to the left of the track, just before the loading dock. Possibly one advantage of starting from

Colchester was that a list of driving details was published a week in advance, so at least the engine crew's leisure time could be pre-planned.

The familiar tender-first train, well recalled in the last steam days, started in 1936 when a simple run round line came into use at Brightlingsea. The engine would draw, right way round, into the Station, detach from the carriages and then, using the run round, join to the rear of the carriages again. It would therefore draw out to Wivenhoe tender first.

The line's stock changed too. In 1936

Hitched up and ready to go. J15 65432 waits for the 'off' to pull a mixed freight train (goods and passengers) to

Colchester in 1956 (*Photo T. E. Rounthwaite*)

the three bogie coaches were replaced by small six wheelers and at the start of the War, the Worsdell J 15 engines were brought to the line, to remain for the rest of its steam days. This goods engine was designed by Thomas Worsdell, whose grandfather had been in at the beginning of railways by designing the water barrel for Stephenson's *Rocket*. They looked far older than 1882 when they were first built, due to their high chimneys looking like a tall Victorian top hat. They were usually black and very dirty with light brown and white staining on their boilers where various chemicals had leaked or boiled out. This was partly brought about, not from loss of pride by drivers and firemen, but by war conditions. The locomotives became a simple all-over black with no fancy lining, the L.N.E.R.

engines being lettered a simple N.E. Engines soon became covered with grime and rust, as the women cleaners who, in the First World War, had usually worked so hard to keep the engines clean, were now urgently needed for industry and more essential war work.

Side windows were fitted to several locomotives plus a windscreen for the tender to eliminate coal dust blowing back on the engine crew when working in tender first position. Langley Aldrich notes that this also made a very effective black-out during the war years.

The term 'Crab and Winkle' which had been given to the line was, at times, used for the earlier Class G 4 engines, but now this tag was given to the J 15s, so much so that you never knew in conversation if the speaker was referring to the engines or the line.

It seemed fitting that these locomotives should come to our line at the start of World War II, for 42 of them had seen service in the mud of Flanders in the First. All were to come back and continue service after wards, except No 513, which was damaged beyond repair and was condemned on 9th August, 1920. She was the first of this Class of 289 locomotives to be scrapped. None of the First World War veterans was among the regulars to be seen on this line.

This class of locomotive had another claim to fame as one of them had made history by breaking all records for British engine construction time.

Naturally, when railway engines began to be built, it was always at the back of the workmen's minds as to how quickly one could be put together. In February, 1888, Crewe Works had constructed a freight engine in 252 hours. Then the record went to America with the Alloona Works of the Pennsylvania Railroad in June of the same year building one in 16¼ hours. Stratford Railway Works was now in full swing and estimated, under normal working conditions, to turn out a new locomotive every 32 hours, so the Great Eastern decided to have a go at the record. On 10th December, 1891, at 9 a.m. 137 men and boys stood ready. All the pieces, over 9,000 for the engine and 7,000 for the tender, lay ready. They had been brought to the assembly point and laid out carefully so as to cause no problems. No attempt had been made to cheat by finding out if they would fit together first, experienced men would know that. The word was given to start, and the gang, 85 on the locomotive and 56 on the tender, went to work at top speed. An

The Westinghouse brake pump shows clearly on J15 65447 working the Colne Valley line (*Photomatic Herts*)

June 1930. Class F4 7219 waits in Brightlingsea Station *(Photo C. Langley Aldrich)*

hour's break was taken for dinner and work ceased at 5.30 p.m., starting again at 6 the next morning. The tender was finished at 7.40 a.m. and the engine at 9.10, the men working on the engine even being allowed to have their customary break between 8.15 and 9. So, after 9 hours and 47 minutes of working time the engine stood ready and before seven that evening had even received her customary coat of grey paint. It was a record never to be broken in steam locomotive production.

After a 30 mile trial trip she went to the running department and then started work hauling coal trains of 560 tons between Peterborough and London. It was to be 36,000 miles later that she was to be spared time to be given her first official coat of paint. This locomotive, No 930 of the Great Eastern, was finally scrapped in 1935, having 'lived' for 46 years and travelled 1,127,750 miles.

As well as the 'Crab and Winkle' nickname one could also add the old favourite of 'fussy little engine', as they were not content to rest silently in the stations awaiting the next task demanded of them, as a constant 'cha-cha' panting came from the Westinghouse Brake Pump, situated on the locomotive side. This steam pump compressed the air which, when allowed to escape, applied the brake automatically. As the fees needed to be paid to the Americans were high, British companies eventually adopted the vacuum brake system. The Great Eastern, however, was even cleverer than that. It would wait for the patent to run out or a new improved version to be introduced, and then use the old version with the expired patent.

This sometimes led them to be 20 years out of date, but it certainly saved money!

These locomotives, after their arrival in 1939, were the only engines, with few exceptions, to run on the branch. In addition to the engines mentioned up to the start of the J 15s, the D 13 4-4-0s could occasionally be seen at the head of a 'mixed' train and rare visitors were the original 'Claud Hamilton' Class up to the time of their rebuilding, which started in 1932. A full list of the line's engines can be found at the back of this book.

The *Gobblers* which, it will be remembered, ran on the branch in the 1910 era, were armour plated in 1941 in anticipation of the expected invasion and could be seen towing anti-tank guns between Thorpe and Walton.

Country station atmosphere at Brightlingsea in the 1950s. Snowball French and Georgie Day are on the locomotive and Johnny Wheeler is the porter. (*Photo Roger Knights*)

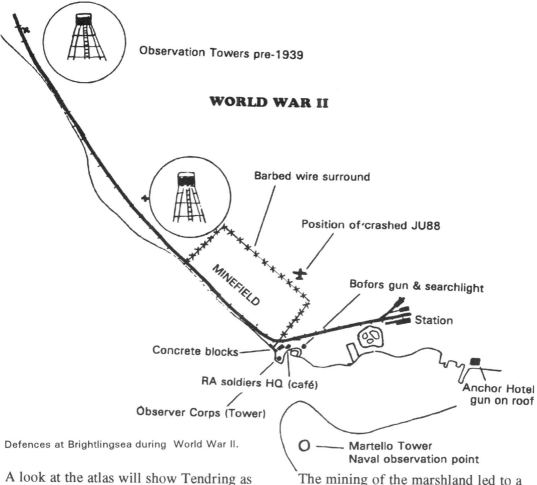

Observation Towers pre-1939

WORLD WAR II

Barbed wire surround

Position of crashed JU88

MINEFIELD

Bofors gun & searchlight

Station

Concrete blocks

RA soldiers HQ (café)

Observer Corps (Tower)

Anchor Hotel gun on roof

Defences at Brightlingsea during World War II.

O —— Martello Tower
Naval observation point

A look at the atlas will show Tendring as one of the most likely places for the expected German seaborne invasion. The Brightlingsea area was quickly defended, a large part of the fields adjoining the railway line from the Promenade to the First Marshes being mined. The beach huts were taken away from the sea front and entry was not permitted without a pass. Even the Swing Bridge was mined and was to be blown up soon as the invasion was confirmed.

The mining of the marshland led to a fatal accident on 5th November, 1940, when two boys were killed. Another who was with them gave this account:

"One afternoon five boys and I decided to go to a barn near a wood on the edge of the marshes close to the railway. While playing in the barn we heard the noise of a shotgun and knew that the gamekeeper was out. After discussion we left the barn as there would have been trouble if we were caught.

The fields to the left were mined in World War Two. One of the last steam runs on the line: the afternoon goods just out from Brightlingsea during the winter of 1959-60. (*Photo author*)

"The marshes had been criss-crossed by deep wide trenches, the idea being to prevent German gliders landing. One boy threw a clod of earth into a trench splashing the others with water. This seemed a good game, so three boys got on each side of the trench and walked along still throwing the dirt. When that trench ended we chose another, but found that it dried up as it neared the barbed wire of the minefield perimeter fence. One of the boys called out that a trench on the other side of the wire was full of water, so we jumped down into the dry trench, crawling under the wire.

"We had only gone a few yards when a mine exploded killing Roy Herbert, whose twin brother was there as well, and Ronald Offord."

At the same time a train was passing. Mr Hawkes, the fireman, heard the explosion and looked out the cab window to see that a mine had gone off and a boy was still in the minefield. In panic, or possibly to look for help, the boy ran right across the minefield to the train embankment, by chance not setting off any other mines.

Meanwhile, Mr Gibson, the game-keeper, had been running after the boys to try to stop them. Being an ex-police sergeant he was able to get the rest of the boys out of the minefield safely and sent two of them tell the police of what had happened. The bodies of two boys were recovered the following day.

The mines had led to other incidents earlier, though not as serious as this. At various times the Royal Observer Corps night watch heard explosions in the minefield as marauding rabbits set them off. The vibrations from this initial explosion would set off other mines and, one night, a total of seven explosions was heard. In early part of the war a bullock was blown to pieces and, as nobody could enter the area to remove the carcase, flocks of rooks would arrive at dawn every day to feast on the remains.

Both Wivenhoe and Brightlingsea were employed to help the naval effort during both World Wars. At Wivenhoe sidings a steam crane was used to load the engines into newly-completed motor torpedo boats. Tanks were unloaded at Wivenhoe to go up to Wivenhoe Park, where there was an Army Parachute Regiment stationed. The Park also contained the body of a disused aircraft for parachute practice.

The Brightlingsea station staff were protected from air attack by a shelter made in the cellar under the station buildings. This proved necessary. 5,500 pontoons for use by the Army were built in the Brightlingsea shipyards and taken by rail. As these were being loaded up an air raid started and German bombers came over, one bomb landing in the field next to the line. Bombs also fell in Promenade Road and, when the raid was over, it was found that machine gun bullets had sprayed the goods' yard.

It was far from being a quiet war at Brightlingsea, although Driver Hawkes was to come closer to danger while driving a train to Walton. Two bombs were dropped which bounced off the railway embankment as the train passed and exploded in an adjoining field.

On a wartime journey to Wivenhoe in early 1940, as the train passed the marshland area by the Long Bridge, the Guard, Jack Lyons, heard the noise of an aircraft flying very low. Looking out of the window he saw a Hurricane coming towards the train and looking as if it would crash into it. It went low over the train and fell into the mud on the seaward side of the track, with only the tail left sticking out. The station staff had watched the Hurricane and the other 'plane, a Messerschmidt 109, crash, both with smoke coming from them. The pilots descended by parachute, the German landing towards Colchester, but the other, a Canadian, walked to Brightlingsea Station and asked to use the telephone. After 'phoning his unit to report the incident, he sat on the station dressed in his flying kit until a truck came to collect him. The remains of his Hurricane are still there, visible at low tide, although they did come to the attention of collectors a few years ago.

Not Mussolini, but Eddie Phillips and 'Andy' Hardy of the Observer Corps on top of Bateman's Tower. The tower has had its 'hat' removed to make aircraft recognition easier (*Photo Alf Jefferies*)

The injured German pilot was found, captured and taken to St Mary's Hospital, Colchester, where his injured leg was amputated. He then sat in bed guarded by soldiers armed with bayonets and ammunition to make sure that he did not escape - on his one leg.

Bateman's Tower was used as an observation point on the sea front. The observation area at the top of the Tower was covered in for protection, but this was quickly removed when it was realised that, although it protected, it also obscured the view out - the very reason it was being used.

At 5.55 on the morning of 3rd October, 1940, just before dawn, Cambridge reported to the Tower that a Beaufort was approaching. Little notice was taken of this Allied aircraft, but when it came overhead it was found to be a German Junkers JU 88 with the markings obliterated. It circled once and then made a perfect wheels up landing, coming to rest only 20 metres from the minefield. The Observers in the Tower rushed across to the 'plane, scrambling across ditches and getting their boots full of mud and water. The soldiers stationed at Brightlingsea got there first and the crew of four, two officers and two airmen, left the aircraft. The officers were ordered to put their hands up, while Mr Andrews, one of the Observers, undid their revolver belts. The rear Gunner asked that he be allowed to go back for his hat, but this was refused. The 'plane itself was only a month old and the markings appeared to have been blacked out only an hour or two before,

the paint being still wet, looking as if the painting had been done with a soaked rag. The crew was marched away in single file to the Police Station, but firstly to the Shipyard, where their braces were taken away to prevent escape. After this they were walked to the Police Station, where they were given a breakfast of bacon and eggs. The injustice of this to their captors, who lived by the Ration Book, is still mentioned today.

Many times an attempt has been made to find out why all this happened, but a satisfactory answer is never forthcoming. Some people thought that the Pilot and crew had been trying to escape to England; others that they had heard that Britain had fallen to the Germans; a third theory was that there had been a mistake in navigation and the crew thought they were over Holland. But why were the markings obliterated? And why was the Pilot so frightened and white with fear after the aircraft had landed? With wartime security, the answers were never given and this incident stays as one of mysteries of the War.

The Observer Corps records and log books show that Brightlingsea took an active part in coastal defence putting to sea to rescue aircrew and keeping a visual search for enemy aircraft. One of the many log book entries reads:

"7 Sept 1942 23.40 Hrs

Enquiry from Brightlingsea Naval base - they confirm that a plane is down in Dengie Flats - nationality unknown - later the Naval Base informs us that the Plane is thought to be hostile. Boats are out, and a search will be made by sea and air in the morning."

Towards the end of the War at 6 p.m. on a Sunday evening a V2 rocket dropped into an area of woodland close to where the J.U.88 had landed and made a crater as big as several buses. The blast hit the Station, knocking flat a Grenadier Guardsman waiting for a train and all the Booking Hall floorboards and papers were blown into the air. Perhaps the V2 best remembered by Brightlingsea locals is that which exploded on re-entry into the atmosphere with a severe explosion early one morning: this woke the town at 7 o'clock and pieces of the rocket fell everywhere. One piece fell on the Station platform and burnt the hands of a porter trying to examine a small wheel from the wreckage.

In Wivenhoe, during a wartime raid, incendiaries rained down on the Marshes and Playing Field in an apparent attempt to hit the shipyards. All signs had been removed from the stations and the familiar cry "Wivna, Wivna" was to disappear for a few years. This also explains why the backs of so many railway benches in the area have a gap in them where the nameplate used to be: it was not the work of vandals or collectors. They were taken away at the start of the War and never returned, to stop identification by low-flying aircraft or invading troops. Those that do exist, Ipswich and Stratford are two, were probably the odd bench that was hidden away in a storeroom.

There were no great defences at Wivenhoe as there were at Brightlingsea, but a searchlight was set up at Fingringhoe. Once more the Wivenhoe folk got their bridge across the river, as a Bailey Bridge was built by the Royal Engineers.

During the War, the guard's vans were of the clerestory type, having been sent to the L.N.E.R. in the mid-30s from the North Eastern region to help them replace their six-wheeler coaches. It would seem that an advantage to the guard was that it had an observation top to enable him to look out, but these were intensely disliked, as they were both draughty and cold. When these continued in service after the War, action was taken to ensure that a cold ride did not re-occur. One evening a chilled guard hooked the van on to the back of parcels run to Newcastle - after all, it was from the North East in the first place - and, with the rest of the Wivenhoe station staff, cheerfully waved it goodbye. Two days later it was back. Newcastle had traced the coach number and the Guard was given a 'more than gentle' talking-to by the Inspector. The other of the two was sort of 'smashed up' one night in the Wivenhoe Sidings. Eventually, about 1950, they left the line forever.

With the ending of the War, the evacuees who had been staying in Brightlingsea returned home, the mines were dug up, and life returned to normal. The timetable the line was now redesigned to fit in with the trains from Colchester and London to enable connections to be made. If it was coming from Colchester, the Brightlingsea train would back into Wivenhoe Sidings, a single piece of track on the down side of

Table 19   COLCHESTER, BRIGHTLINGSEA, FRINTON-ON-SEA, WALTON-ON-NAZE, and CLACTON-ON-SEA

The war timetable for early 1945.

the station at the Colchester end, and the passengers would have to wait till the connection arrived. You could, if it was autumn and you were on the school train, jump down on to the track, run into the woods and collect chestnuts while your pals would shout to you if the train was likely to start or if 'Chopper', the Wivenhoe porter, was about. This was fun, but not so a long wait on a winter's night when you wanted to get home.

With the Brightlingsea connections, the trains to Colchester would have to be held up should they not arrive on time. This caused an enquiry to be held shortly after the War concerning a guard on the Brightlingsea train. As the train, the 5.15 from Brightlingsea, started on its journey across the Marshes on a June evening in 1947 it was stopped by a man waving his arms. He and a girl had been jumping the fleets on the marshland when she fell and broke a leg. Mr Lyons, the guard and a part-time ambulance man, left the train to give assistance. This held up the trains on the entire route to London and an enquiry had to be held. It showed the fear of railway employees for the Rule Book, when Mr Lyons concluded his statement, "Again, I regret the delay of the train, but trust I did the right thing under the circumstances..." The girl was married with her right leg still in plaster and Mr Lyons attended the wedding.

In 1946, the numbering of the line's J 15s began to change in preparation for nationalisation two years later, when the London and North Eastern Railway became a part of British Railways.

A view across to Brightlingsea from Point Clear, St Osyth, the curve showing how closely the railway ran beside the river. A two car diesel railcar can be seen behind the Brightlingsea promenade. 1950s postcard.

Aerial View, Brightlingsea   PN3406

NATIONALISATION

Local L.N.E.R. numbers had been from 7001 upwards: it will be recalled that they had simply added 7000 to the locomotives inherited from the Great Eastern, quite straightforward method of identifying the former company and, to some extent, what area a locomotive came from or the time of manufacture. Now all this was to change and bore no resemblance to what had gone before. The Regions were allocated a number from 1,000 to 69,999 - Eastern Region being 60,00 to 69,999. Locomotives were then sorted out as near possible into class order and date of manufacture. Then the classes were shaped within a number framework, larger passenger engines first, then mixed traffic and freight, tank engines coming last. For a period after re-numbering, before the final 6 was added to the front, the prefix letter E was used. The full L.N.E.R. lettering had

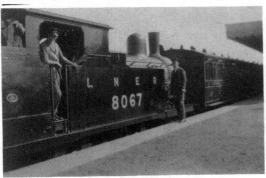

L.N.E.R. 8067 stands in Brightlingsea Station in the 1930s (*Photo C. Langley Aldrich*)

returned in 1946, replacing the N.E. of war years. Shortly after nationalisation the words 'British Railways' appeared on the tender or tank sides, later to be replaced by the British Railways' emblem.

Luckily for train spotters, the most familiar locomotives that now ran on the branch, the J 15s, had numbers that seemed to run in sequence or could be easily remembered, 65432, 65444 and 65448, for example.

Carriages had become corridor stock made up of three coach sets for normal runs. Once again the engine shed was brought into use, although not for overnight stops.

Passenger traffic was high and, on one day in 1952, 1,600 passengers used the train, the total for the year being 30,000. Additionally, one and a half million oysters were carried each year in the 6 years following nationalisation. The passenger traffic was so large on summer Sundays or Bank Holidays that the train stretched from the buffers to the very end of the platform at Brightlingsea, meaning that the locomotive was unable to use the run-round loop. A stand-by engine had to be brought out of the Shed to take the train out and the remaining locomotive would now enter the Shed to perform the same operation with the next train in.

Some trains ran from Brightlingsea to Wivenhoe only to form a connection

An aerial view of Brightlingsea station taken in 1963 (*Photo Alf Jefferies*)

J15 65424 waits in Colchester St Botolph's on 3rd September, 1956, about to depart with a train for Brightlingsea. (*Photo T. E. Rounthwaite*)

service. Others went to Colchester Main Station (North) via St Botolph's, where the locomotive once again had to run round the train. Early morning or late afternoon trains tended to be of this type to enable businessmen, workers and schoolchildren reach Colchester in under 20 minutes. A wait in the Wivenhoe sidings on the other trains could mean that the same journey took an hour. The local bus service took 50 minutes.

Look beyond the points at Brightlingsea Station and Hygene Cottage marks the site of the sewage works. It was here that the 1953 flood first made itself known.

'Chopper' Hatch, the Wivenhoe porter, soon solved the problem of the Wivenhoe sidings for sailors and friends between the hours of 6 and 10 at night, although it cost you the occasional drink. There was no need to wait sitting in a cold train in the sidings, you could go into the *Station* Hotel across the road for a drink and 'Chopper' would tell you when the train came in and it certainly couldn't leave until he gave it the right of way. This service is remembered with affection by the Brightlingsea bargemen, who had come across from the sandpit workings at Rowhedge and had a long wait for the train.

Camping coaches were brought to Brightlingsea. This was an idea by British Railways, when coaches, converted into sleeping accommodation, were brought to seaside resorts. Pulled by a locomotive, often as part of a train, they were sited by the water column at the end of Brightlingsea Station.

The sea, having been quiet for a while, flooded the line again in early April, 1949. One Monday the 11.02 a.m. from Brightlingsea was unable to return. Beach huts were washed away from their sites and one caravan was surrounded by water, the occupants having to escape through the roof. The line was closed for a time and a bus service was brought in to take passengers to Wivenhoe. This was considered to be a serious flood, but the sea was only practising.

Hygene Cottage has an interesting name for a cottage at the entrance to a sewage works on a low-lying marsh. Shortly after midnight on 1st February, 1953, Mr Green went outside the cottage to tend his pigs, taking his son with him. Searchlights had been set up on the Promenade by the police, who were there, waiting. The high tide at Lowestoft at 8 p.m. had given an indication that the situation was serious.

All at once Mr Green looked up to see a wall of water from a giant flood wave approaching. The full force of it hit him, almost taking him off his feet, and leaving him up to his shoulders in water. Shouting to his son to go indoors to see if all was well, he managed to find a boat and eventually, with piglets swimming behind his craft, he reached the house.

Where the sea burst through at Wivenhoe. Its ballast washed away, the track hangs in mid-air.

The flood has come to Wivenhoe marshes during the night of 31st January - 1st February 1953.

135

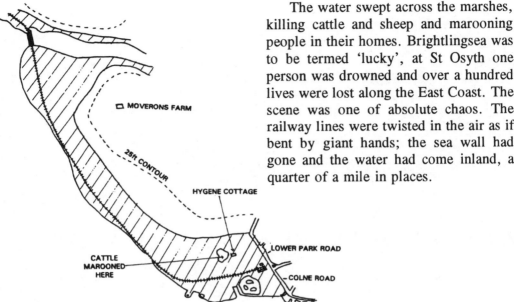

MOVERONS FARM

25ft CONTOUR

HYGENE COTTAGE

LOWER PARK ROAD

COLNE ROAD

CATTLE MAROONED HERE

The extent of the flooding at Brightlingsea

The water swept across the marshes, killing cattle and sheep and marooning people in their homes. Brightlingsea was to be termed 'lucky', at St Osyth one person was drowned and over a hundred lives were lost along the East Coast. The scene was one of absolute chaos. The railway lines were twisted in the air as if bent by giant hands; the sea wall had gone and the water had come inland, a quarter of a mile in places.

One of his sows was to be found many days later wandering dejectedly by the edge of the flood waters almost a mile from home, apparently having swum to safety. Mrs Green first knew of the flood when the front door was smashed in by the flood water and Grandfather, who they were sure was drowned, was to be found still asleep while his bed bumped against the ceiling. There is something to be said for wooden beds.

The flood had come, which was to be called 'the worst disaster in the town's history' by local reporter, Len Southern. A strong wind blowing south-ward had driven a storm surge into the funnel-shaped North Sea. Added to this it was the time of the high Spring Tide and heavy rainfall had produced swollen rivers to aid these other factors.

Removing the stranded trucks from Brightlingsea Station following temporary repairs to the line following the 1953 flooding (*Photo Essex County Newspapers*)

Brightlingsea, the Saxon name for which was Beortric's Island, was an island again. One farmer, Mr Girling, had to row out to feed his cattle, stranded on a small piece of land that stood up like an islet. He eventually drove them through the water back to their sheds using a rowing boat, a trick, it was said, he had learned while in Australia.

When the sea subsided and the land was pumped dry the situation for the railway seemed impossible. Over the marshland 50 sheep lay scattered; we would jump on the carcasses to get them to bleat, and many of the trees had rabbits hanging from their branches, like some kind of macabre fruit, following their being carried by the flood waters.

At first it was decided that the line would not re-open. This was followed by a public meeting held with the railway authorities in the Brightlingsea New Church Hall in Queens Street. The Eastern National Bus Company operated a new service that connected with the train at Wivenhoe. However, as they had done before, the Brightlingsea people fought to have the line restored.

Mr Charles Johnson, with 37 years experience on the railway, took up the cause. A body was set up by the Government to hear the argument the meeting was held at Liverpool Street, where, on the morning of the enquiry, 9th June, 1953, the Tuesday after the Coronation, the caretaker set out four chairs and a small table expecting, as usually happened in these cases, the local parson and the parish clerk. He had underestimated the spirit of the Brightlingsea folk; forty or more people arrived in angry mood.

Plenty of argument was put forth. The Chairman, Mr Hines, reported that the closure of the line would save the railways £8,709 per year, although nobody was able to find out how such an accurate sum had been arrived at! Freight was the best argument against closure and 80% of this was fish traffic. Oyster freight had recently made a dramatic increase and were making quite a profitable industry for the small town. 60,000 a year in 1948 had now reached 250,000 in 1952. They went off quickly, the Committee was told, and transport by road meant them being stacked 6 baskets high, as opposed to 3 on the trains, thus saving considerable damage to the lower baskets, as occurred when they were moved by road.

Two of the Board's members were railway officials, one of whom argued the railway's case, and then sat on the Committee to judge it. At the end of three days' argument the Chairman closed the case, but Mr Johnson wasn't having that. He brought the Chairman down to Brightlingsea to hear the complaints of the people themselves.

The arguments raged all summer. Brightlingsea Carnival in August saw a huge replica of the 'Crab and Winkle' driven round the Recreation Ground. 'The Ghost Train' was written on the engine, with 'Will ye no...' to express public feeling on the side. Following this was a large paper tortoise, 'Why worry - no train' was the notice it carried.

The Central Transport Users'

Consultative Committee sat at Cardiff on 13th October and decided to give the line a three year trial, during which time the road between Brightlingsea and Thorrington was to be widened; it seemed as if they planned the reopening as a temporary measure. The road widening was never carried out, possibly because the cost would have been rather greater than the upkeep of the railway.

After extensive repairs, the line reopened on 7th December, 1953. The first train out, J 15, number 65448, consisting of 4 carriages with 51 passengers, drew out in the darkness at 6.40 a.m., the platform being full of people, even at that early hour of a winter's morning. As the train left the station, a loud roar came from fog detonators placed on the line by Mr Condor, the Station Master. I went on that first train and was caught up in the excitement of the occasion. The trains tended to come back almost immediately from Wivenhoe, then wait at Brightlingsea, so I came back on the return train, had a quick breakfast, and then went off to school on the next train out.

Almost a carnival atmosphere existed for the rest of the day, and so there should have been! It was one of the few times that a line had been reopened by the united efforts of the passengers themselves.

The children arrive on the afternoon of 7th December, 1953, for a free train ride to celebrate the re-opening after the floods (*East Anglian Film Archive*)

An L.M.S. Ivatt, a visitor to the line, gets decorated (*East Anglian Film Archive*)

At 1.20 230 children from the Primary School had a free ride to Colchester. Councillor Fensom, the Deputy Mayor, conducted the children in the singing of 'God save the Queen' in the Goods' Yard before the train's departure. There is strong evidence to suggest that he paid for the outing, but didn't want the fact known. The train was decked with flags and cheers, bells and whistles followed the train along its route. It arrived at Wivenhoe to be greeted by lines of schoolchildren who had been let out of class to see the Crab and Winkle running once more. At Wivenhoe Station, Councillor Polly spoke of the fact that his grandfather had ridden in the cab of the first train some 90 years before. East Anglian Film Archives

possess a film of the train's departure from Brightlingsea. A celebration dance was held that night in the Scouts' Hall at Brightlingsea followed by a late train back to Colchester at 12.15 a. m.

If ever there was a 'finest hour' in the history of the line, this was it, and yet time was running out. No one at the celebrations would have dreamt that the line had only 11 years to go.

In the years that followed the school-boys continued their usual pranks on the porters, but no matter what they did, nothing was so memorable as the night of 26th November, 1954. As the 5.40 train to Brightlingsea approached the Swing Bridge the vacuum brake was applied to bring the speed down to 5 m.p.h. Unfortunately the brake was not released

The train arrives at Wivenhoe on a dull December afternoon, but the line is re-opened again

The muddy surrounds of the Swing Bridge into which Mr Sycamore fell on 26th November, 1954.

in time and the train stopped on the bridge. It was a terrible night of driving rain and almost no visibility. Mr Sycamore, a Colchester businessman, seeing the bridge light, assumed the train was in the station. Putting down the book he was reading and picking up his umbrella, he stepped out of the compartment, over the side of the bridge and, after a fall of 20 feet, went into the mud below. The driver, 'Ezzy' Hawkes, saw him go and the train remained halted while he was hauled out of the mud with the aid of a rope and up the rocks to the side of the track. Before the train arrived at Brightlingsea Station, although he had been sorted out as much as possible, Mr Sycamore, feeling rather self-conscious of his muddy condition and the fact that this was a crowded train of fellow commuters, asked the Guard, Mr Lyons, if he could remain behind until all the men had left the station. A good idea in theory, but all it did was to give the group around the ticket barrier time to get a better view. He was then helped home by two of the station staff. Apart from shock and a pair of broken glasses he was alright but, as one of the staff commented, "Thank God it was low tide!" It was to be a long time before the incident was forgotten. At the Christmas Fancy Dress Party held at the Brightlingsea Sailing Club, attended by the victim, sure enough, there was a local joker in bowler hat and business suit with seaweed poking out of every pocket.

J15 65468 leaves the Swing Bridge on the Wivenhoe side in May, 1956 (*Photo Dr Ian C. Allen*)

The Swing Bridge was often used by people walking to and from Wivenhoe. Sometimes they carried timetables in their pockets to avoid meeting a train halfway across. It was very easy in a headwind for a train to come very close to you before you realised it was there and, as children, there was always the fear of the dreaded £5 (a hundred weeks' pocket-money!) fine mentioned on all the notices that, so the signs said, would be taken from anyone caught trespassing on the railway. Actually, the shock of a train whistle from right behind you gave more than five pounds-worth of fright, especially as you could not see the train crew grinning as they did it. We always believed that the driver carried a roll of £5 tickets for just such occasions as when he caught one of us.

Bridge crossing was an old occupation for children since before the Second World War. The plan used by the waiting children to cross the bridge was simple, at least from the Wivenhoe side. On a summer's night the Bridge Pilot would sit in his chair at the cottage doorway and, on hot evenings, his head would drop slowly forward as he nodded off to sleep. When a brave lad, watching for these tell-tale signs, found that he had, in fact, dropped off he and his friends would crawl slowly forwards on their hands and knees until the safety of the Bridge was reached: then it was a mad scramble for the Brightlingsea side. It was not so easy to get back though.

Crawling seemed to be a part of railway games, another of which was "Hide in First" on the school train. This simply meant to ride in splendour in the first class compartments from St Botolph's and hide in the toilets to avoid being seen at Wivenhoe. Should anyone come into the first class section at Wivenhoe, then you were in trouble, as you then had to crawl past their compartment in order to avoid being seen. Actually it was more of a dirty slither on the stomach, until an empty compartment was gained. Once, while intently engaged in doing this, an elderly lady slid back her compartment door and stepped straight on to my back: I am still not sure who was the more shocked.

Rumour had it that Roman coins could be found under the Swing Bridge and we searched for hours, getting only cut feet from glass and oyster shells. I once found a real Roman spear in splendid condition and treasured it carefully, but now I can recognise an old boat hook when I see one!

We knew for sure that visitors used to throw coins out as the train passed over the bridge, a tradition carried out

This is how it always looked in the days of steam. The regular J15 locomotive with its three carriages crosses the wooden bridge (*Photo Alf Jefferies*)

over many bridges and having its origins, not in the days of steam locomotives, but in pagan man trying to keep the water sprites happy.

On our final day at school, when we were at last free to enter the world as men on our last journey home on the train, we used to throw our school caps into the waters of Alresford Creek. I can still remember the purple cap that I had hated having to wear for so long, sinking beneath the grey, muddy water.

Hiding under the Wooden Bridge when the train went overhead was another dangerous schoolboy game. The Bridge was only 6 feet high and used to groan and bend with the enormous weight, 67 tons, of the engine and tender

passing just over our heads. The sport came to a sudden end when someone above decided to pull the toilet flush!

Coins tied to the track was another pastime that everyone has heard of - slow goods trains were best for really large discs, expresses just shot your coin off somewhere with the first wheel, but an elderly lady assured me that crossed dressmaking pins turn into a lovely pair of scissors for use as a broach.

Between 1951 and 1957 several Ivatt 2-6-0 tender engines of the L.M.S. Region were used on the line, smart with black and red lining. These had been re-allocated to the Eastern Region, but the line had far fewer of them than had been anticipated, as they were used mainly on the Marks Tey to Cambridge route.

These were about the biggest engines the line could take. Even when the *Claud* locomotive had run here many years earlier there were fears of its only trip doing damage to the line and its bridges - it was 51 tons as opposed to the J 15s 37 tons. There was a rumour in the early 50s that a *Britannia* Class locomotive ran once, but, as usual, nobody remembers actually seeing it, but always know that 'somebody' did, although this class of locomotive did certainly run on the first quarter mile of track before branching off on the Walton line. Built too late in the days of steam to realise their full potential, these green and black locomotives with distinctive chime (siren) and

windshields, started work on the Clacton business trains on 9th June, 1958. Electrification was to come to the line on 13th April, 1959.

With these changing years came another locomotive to the line, the J 69s, which had been far more used in the London Suburban services. First built in 1890, the three most frequent visitors to the branch, where they helped in the Goods Yard, were 68573, 77 and 78.

From the 1950s onwards a high proportion of L.N.E.R. stock appeared. including flushed steel panelled vehicles, while the occasional British Railways coach was in evidence before the coming railcar era.

On 4th March, 1957, the diesel

The view never to be the same again. Electrification came to Wivenhoe on 13th April, 1959, but steam continues to survive for a few months yet. Taken on 2nd August, 1959. (*Photo A. E. Bennett*)

143

The first day of the diesel railcars, 4th March, 1957. The Stationmaster, Mr Condor, hands the staff to Driver Barnes. The tall silhouette in the carriage is the author! (*Photo East Anglian Daily Times*)

railcars or D.M.U.s (Diesel Multiple Units) as they were more properly called, came and took over the passenger services. The attraction of these was, and still is for children, that if a front or rear seat was obtained (we fought furiously for these on the school trains) a clear view was given of the track through the glass partitions behind the cabs - after first making sure that you had not got a seat behind the driver, otherwise your view would be of a swaying black jacket. It was also possible to watch the speed indicator to see if he would ever do 'more than seventy' and a rev counter or, as we thought of it, a very efficient dial which told him when he needed to change gear, was situated on the instrument panel.

Metro Cammell D.M.U. at Brightlingsea Station (*Photo Winston Cole*)

144

The conversion training from steam to diesel for the drivers took only two weeks, one week in the classroom and another week's experience. These later became pay trains and tickets were bought from the guard. The J 15s were relegated to the goods runs and were finally phased out.

The goods finally ceased to be drawn by steam in May, 1960, but until then the J 15s or J 69s still hauled the afternoon goods leaving Wivenhoe at 3.20 on weekdays, arriving in Brightlingsea at 3.35. It left again at 4.03 to get back to Wivenhoe 15 minutes later.

Steam was slowly beginning to go from the area. The 'old faithful' of the line, 65432, was withdrawn from service in 1958 and 65424 a year later. At the start of the 50s Colchester Sheds were responsible for 67 steam locomotives; by December, 1959, the number had dropped to 24 and within the next five months steam was to go forever.

THE DIESELS

With the arrival of the evening Continental Boat train at Liverpool Street on Sunday, 10th September, 1962, steam went from East Anglia, except for a small area around Peterborough and March. The white streams of smoke splitting the woods and fields was finished. What was the attraction of steam? Why did children feel an affection for a machine, which in any other form would probably have terrified them? There have been many theories put forward. I believe these engines gave out a noise not far removed from human breathing and, with their size and power, they were to mankind of the 19th and 20th centuries what the Gods had been to primitive man.

Things were slowly changing and slowing down all round us. Thorrington Station had closed to passenger and parcel traffic on 4th November, 1957.

The first diesel railcars were Metropolitan Cammell manufactured, although these were occasionally replaced by the Wickhams Company units. As with steam locomotives, there is a special language to be learnt when discussing the diesels: carriages were termed 'cars' and two cars made a unit or set. A unit normally ran on the line, with two units - 4 cars - for the busy summer traffic.

A skilful method was used to ensure regular servicing. B Perren, writing in *Trains Illustrated* explains: The units were kept at Ipswich, whence they would spend a single day on the Brightlingsea branch, leaving Ipswich on the 5.18 a.m. to Colchester and then start their day's work to and from Brightlingsea, starting

A Derby lightweight rattles past Brightlingsea promenade. (*Photo Alf Jefferies*)

at 6.01 and finishing at 10.34 p.m. The next day the units would start a different area of working, bringing it closer and closer to Norwich for eventual servicing after a period of two weeks. Then it would start off again and work its way back to Ipswich.

Later, the Derby Lightweights, made by a local firm in Bishop's Stortford, were to take over from the previous units and, in 1959, these were to be replaced by the Cravens unit, which was to stay until the end of the line. These Cravens can still be seen on the Marks Tey to Sudbury route at the time of writing, so it is still just possible to get some of the atmosphere of the latter days of the line.

If this information about various units is confusing to the non-technical reader, there is a way of recognising the differing types. The Derby Lightweights had three front windows and the others two. The Wickhams had a dome-shaped top to its front, the Metro Cammell had a sloping front, while the Cravens had two windows and is that still seen in service today: I hope that clarifies the matter slightly.

For goods work, now that steam had finally gone, the Drury Diesel Shunter was used, D2209 being a regular. Later came the Hunslett Shunter, recognisable by the manufacturer's name on its front.

In the early 60s a rather difficult feat was performed with an early morning diesel run: after leaving Brightlingsea the leading car's instruments failed, so the driver drove the train backwards from the rear end of the train. Approaching Wivenhoe Junction the Guard sat in the front driving position, using the bell to indicate the position of the signals. Happy ignorance of the passengers!

Despite new engines and timetables, the speed of the journey had changed little since 1920. The trip to Wivenhoe took 13 minutes then and 10 in 1960. The journey to London, two and a half hours when the line opened, took one hour, fifty-one minutes in 1920 and just over one and a half hours in 1960.

The country station atmosphere went when the steam trains left. There is no doubt that they were part of the homely feeling that existed at Brightlingsea Station. To give late-comers a warning the lights were flicked on and off on a dark winter's morning to show that the train was about to start and the guard would walk through the Booking Hall and look up the road to see if anyone was coming before waving the train out.

Two late 'specials' would arrive just in time on cycles and the staff would have a friendly bet as to who would be the last. It was not unknown for the train to back into the station to collect somebody who had 'nearly made it '.

Shoppers, however, were to find the trains difficult when wanting to go to Colchester for just a few hours, as all the trains ran to coincide with connections elsewhere. This meant that there was no regular interval between train times. Coming back from school, had I missed the 4.15 from St Botolph's, I had to wait until 5.40 for the next. On a winter's night with a hot tea waiting at home, it was heartbreaking to find that you had just missed the train. A few times I chased after the rear of the train, only to find it slowly drawing away from me. I would then collapse against a wall crying, both from frustration and the thought of the long wait ahead.

For the passengers an interest in the seaward side of the track started at this time due to various unusual visitors. A seal could be seen regularly at the Swing Bridge and, in October, 1963, a 40 foot whale was washed ashore near the Wooden Bridge. It was buried by the local council, but washed free again. It was towed out to sea and released - but it came back! Finally in desperation, it was cut up and taken to the local rubbish tip, by way of the town. This final act is still remembered, if only because of the smell!

CLOSURE

The final closure of the line was sudden and unpredicted Dr Beeching, the Chairman of British Rail, decided that, for reasons of finance and due to many of smaller lines not making a profit, hundreds of branch lines, some among the most beautiful stretches of railway in Britain, must be closed. The Brightlingsea Branch was on the list. What arguments could be put forward?

Even in 1947, in an issue of *Railway Pictorial,* there had been criticism of the line. The writer stated the bus fare was half that of the railway - 1/4d, as opposed to 2/8d. Traffic was very low, he continued, in fact a one-car diesel service could easily replace the 'very generous' engine and three coaches. But there no doubt it was high fares that kept local folk off the branch and, was there to be a return to cheap fares and full holiday facilities at Brightlingsea, the crowds would return to the railway.

The 2,000 visitors of August Monday, 1938, had long gone. The population had grown little, from 4,501 in 1901 - the year the old station had burnt down - to 4,801 in 1961.

D I Gordon suggests that it was too much in the shadow of Clacton to hold its own as an attractive holiday resort for the 'two week summer holiday' man or the London day tripper. By 1963 only 600 passengers a day were using the railway and two-thirds of these were concentrated on 6 of the 30 daily trains.

Mr Cox, the Brightlingsea porter, said of the situation, "So the position was that, with the loss of sprat, shrimp and oyster traffic and the closure of one of the shipyards, the only remaining traffic consisted of workmen and shop-assistants who travelled up on the first three trains in the morning and about fifty or sixty children attending school in Colchester, plus about thirty commuters to London and back."

The severe winter of 1962/3 almost wiped out the oyster trade and the trains at certain times of the day ran almost empty. On the Sunday evening trains there were sometimes only one or two passengers and the guard.

However, once again the fight to save the line was taken up. Why not? It had been done before, in 1906 when it was closed due to flooding, in 1923 because of the cost of the bridge, and in 1953 after the floods. So it could be kept open once more.

The *Essex County Standard* of July, 1963, carried the following Public Notice

"Withdrawal of Railway Passenger Services.

The Eastern Region of British Railways hereby give notice in accordance with Section 56 (7) of the Transport Act of 1962, that on and from 4th Nov 1963 they propose to discontinue services between Wivenhoe and Brightlingsea, and from the following station - BRIGHTLINGSEA."

There was an application for objections within six weeks. We weren't accepting that, an objection was made. Mr French, a member of Brightlingsea Council, took up the fight that might well be the last. British Railways stated that numbers using the line had dwindled with the years and that it had become an uneconomic proposition. They estimated that, at the moment, earnings for the line were £8,000, expenditure £18,000, with an extra £10,000 needed over the following five years for the replacement of worn-out equipment.

Mr French argued back, pointing out the cold of winter bus travel, the convenience of the train for mothers with prams, and the facilities for goods traffic. Petitions were raised from school-children, shopkeepers and fishermen, and

Mr Reg French, the line's champion, is on the right. The Councillor who was to fight so hard, but in vain, for the saving of the line. Seen here with two local M.P.s and Snowball French, the driver, during the re-opening following the 1953 floods. (*Photo Evening Gazette*)

people were encouraged to use the line. Sadly, this had little effect.

The service had had a run-down look about it in recent years. Most of the journeys to and from Colchester involved changing at Wivenhoe, either to or from the Clacton or Walton trains and waiting for a connection. Anyone having a night out in Colchester was always forced to get the bus home, as the last train, except for Saturdays, left Wivenhoe for Brightlingsea at 9 p.m.

A keen watch was kept on passenger totals to support the case against British Railways, but on 15th October, 1963, Mr Peck of Wivenhoe 'phoned Mr French, "Trouble on the railway last Friday. Did three runs, thought you might like to know about them

Friday 1st run (6.55 p.m.)
   21passengers down; 5 back
  2nd run   13 down: 5 back
   3rd run   7 down: 4 back
Saturday   1st run (1.15 p.m.)
  5 down: 30 back
  2nd run   6 down: 5 back."

So it can be seen that the appeal for people to use the line was just not working. The case for the closure of the line was a good one, but the intended closure date of 4th November passed. People rose in support in literary style. A reporter on the *Colchester Express* of 18th April, 1963, had written, "When the sun shines - glinting on the Colne on one side, and the natural woodland on the other - it is well worth a ride on the little diesel cars that now cover the route, just to stare out of the window."

In March, 1964, the Minister of Transport, Ernest Marples, stipulated that a bus service must be set up to cover closed railway lines, and so the Eastern National began a new service, No. 74, to connect with Wivenhoe and Colchester stations. This journey took 23 minutes compared with the 45 minutes taken by the existing bus service. However, the first bus in the morning was not early enough to equal the 6.07 Colchester to Brightlingsea early morning special, which returned to Wivenhoe at 6.35.

The station staff got many letters from railway collectors who seemed to sense that the closure was imminent. They seemed to want not only tickets, but anything bearing the name 'Brightlingsea'.

The fight continued, but a new closure date was given - 14th June, 1964. Mr French was finding it difficult as the only way that closure could be opposed was on hardship, which was very difficult to define.

14th June arrived. It was a sunny evening, as it had been a sunny day when they had opened the line 98 years previously.

David Winnick, the Labour candidate for the Harwich constituency, was there and pledged, "If a Labour Government gets re-elected in October, we will ask a Labour Minister of Transport to re-open the line." Labour supporters handed out a yellow pamphlet to all the passengers telling of their promises. It reflected the line's history and commented that things might have been better had certain improvements been made during the line's existence. A rail siding could have connected with industrial sites near the Hard. A halt could have been made at Alresford Creek with a goods siding for the local sandpit. "A scandal and a shame are the only words to describe the closure of the Railway" the pamphlet concluded.

Harold Bloes was to be the driver of the last train. He had worked on the Brightlingsea line for 45 years. In the cab window was a notice which said simply "Last Train R.l.P."

And finally... The last train prepares to leave on the evening of Sunday, 14th June, 1964. Harold Blois the driver. (*Photo Essex County Newspapers*)

150

Sunday 7.30 p.m., 14th June, 1964 after 98 years of service, the last train prepares to leave. The boy in the front holds a Labour Party leaflet, promising to re-open the line if they are elected. (*Photo G.R. Mortimer*)

The train, the usual two-car diesel, was packed and several hundred people watched the departure, including press photographers and one man with a tape recorder. It left at 7.30 to the sound of fog detonators placed under the wheels and, ironically, the last time they had been used for such a purpose was in 1953 for the joyful re-opening after the floods.

The small train pulled away into the bright low evening sun and rounded the curve and away across the marsh. It was watched until it disappeared behind a clump of trees and would not be seen again. The people on the station turned and walked away and there was a strange sort of silence as they left the station and walked home. Not much was said, there was not much to say.

The track was still there, however, so there was still hope that it could be re-opened, but, several years after the finish, Mr French said, in his usual honest fashion, "We knew by the attitude of the people we were dealing with in London that they had no intention of retaining the line."

Julian Ridsdale, M.P., wrote on 21st October, asking the Minister to reconsider his decision in respect of places where the track had not been torn up. It was later to be found that British Railways had, one week before on 14th October, given the contract for the lifting of the sleepers to L Fairclough of London. There should have been a three year delay before this happened, so all the promises made to Mr Ridsdale in connection with the line's re-opening were worthless and, understandably, he was very angry about the whole affair.

On 11th November, on a misty Wednesday morning, workmen started

The removal of the track four months after closure - November, 1954. It should have remained in place for three years in case of a reprieve. (*Photo Essex County Newspapers*)

pulling up the track by removing the wooden blocks and shoes holding the line. The rail itself was cut by welding equipment and lifted clear of the track by a tractor.

The *Essex County Standard* of 18th November commented, "One part of the line will remain. The Swing Bridge will not be demolished, but left permanently open to allow shipping to pass." But, in 1967, three years after closure, it was demolished, leaving a gap like a drawn tooth between the Brightlingsea and Wivenhoe sides of the Creek. For all the Brightlingsea people's fears of the bridge collapsing, the concrete stumps forming the pivot at the centre of the bridge had to be blown up with explosives.

Labour were to remain true to their promise made on that final evening. Two years after closure, just before the demolition of the bridge, the Harwich branch of the party sent a resolution to Mrs Barbara Castle, Minister of Transport, asking for the line to be re-opened,

one point being that Brightlingsea Council had just undertaken the development of 700 new homes in the town. At the same time the Essex River Authority requested that the railway embankments be handed over to them, as they wished to turn them into much needed additional sea defences. As the track had been taken up, it was the River Authority that got its way.

The Wooden Bridge was partly demolished at this time, as it was thought to be causing erosion.

The Brightlingsea Station was left standing, but, as British Railways were slow in selling the property to Brightlingsea Council, who were anxious to buy it, it became a playground for children, who set fire to it, resulting in the local fire brigade being called out on several occasions. After a serious fire it was demolished in 1968 and on the site there now stands a Community Centre.

Wivenhoe Signal Box was abolished on 23rd July, 1967, and all the Wivenhoe signals became controlled from East Gates on the up line and Thorpe on the down.

Of the many odd things that remain to this day, the *Station* Hotel, Wivenhoe, still sells the Tolly Cobbold beer it did when the line was opened.

The Wivenhoe side of Alresford Creek still looks as if a railway ran there: there is a wide cinder footpath near the Creek, but nearer Wivenhoe, due to people thinking it was still a footpath (which it wasn't) it has been heavily fortified with ditches and barbed wire to keep people out.

Brightlingsea Station before demolition in the Summer of 1967 (*Photo author*)

It is still said locally that the line should have been kept. I would like to agree - but can't! Brightlingsea has expanded away from the station and the Swing Bridge would have to be looked after and checked. The sea waits and will come again, as every 25 years or so it seems to... 1953... 1928... 1904...

Mostly it has all gone now, but there are memories... The smell of steam and smoke... Noisy slamming of doors...

Cries of "Wiv'noe, Wiv'noe, change here for Colchester and Lunnon" and "Brightlingsea train only"... Condensation running down the windows and leather straps on the doors... Differing wheel sounds on the Wooden and Swing Bridges... Children waving from the Promenade... Dog roses on the Station... The rush for the ticket barrier... All gone...

SIGNIFICANT DATES

1860	28 April	Lord of Manor rights obtained
1861	11 July	Act of Parliament granted
1863	8 May	Hythe-Wivenhoe section opened
1863	21 September	Turning of the First Sod Ceremony
1866	17 April	Line opens
1876	August	W & B R C go independent
1879	1 September	Great Eastern operate again
1893	1 August	Great Eastern take over
1901	30 December	Brightlingsea Station burnt down
1904	30 December	Serious flooding. Threatened closure
1906	3 September	New Brightlingsea Station opened
1923	1 January	L.N.E.R. take over operation
1948	1 January	British Railways take over operation
1953	31 January	East Coast Flood. Line closed
1953	7 December	Line re-opened
1957	4 March	Diesel railcars take over passenger traffic
1960	May	Last steam run on line
1964	14 June	Line closed
1964	11 November	Track begins to be lifted

ENGINES OF THE LINE

The run round loop at Brightlingsea. Locomotive J15 65468 passes its carriages to return, and hitch onto the front. A photograph taken in the early 1950s.

1866-1870	Sinclair 2-4-2T Passenger Tank ?
1870-1877	Johnson 0-4-2T Light Branch ?
	Adams 0-4-2T K 9 ?
1877-1879	Hudswell Clarke 184 (*Resolute* No. 1)
1879-189?	As 1870-7
189?-1906	Intermediate T 26 (E4)
1906-1910	M 15 *'Gobbler'*
1910-1914	Y 65 *'Crystal Palace'*
1914-1919	1100 Class S 44
1919-1925	Y 65 *'Crystal Palace'*
[1924-1928]	No 8314 (No 5 C.V.& H.R.)
1925-1939	8040 F 3 Occasional D 13, D14, D15
1939-1957[60]	Worsdell Y 14 (J15)
[1951-1957]	Ivatt 2-6-0 L.M.S.
[1957-1960]	Holden J 69
1957-1958	Metro-Cammell D.M.U. Possibly Wickhams D. M. U.
1958-1960	Derby Lightweight D.M.U.
1960-1964	Cravens D.M.U.

SIGNAL BOXES

Wivenhoe Station Signal Box
Built Autumn, 1886: closed 23rd July, 1967.
13'0" x 25'6" x 8'0" Brick construction
Built by Mckensie & Holland
5" frame   31 levers: 21 working; 10 spare
Note: No details remain of the previous separate box that stood at the Brightlingsea end of the Station from 1863 to 1886.

Wivenhoe Junction Signal Box
Built July, 1898: closed 17th July, 1938.
11'6" x 18'6" x 8'0" Wood construction Built by Evans O'Donnell
4" frame 20 levers: 14 working; 6 spare

Brightlingsea Station Signal Box (1)
Built 1866: closed 1906?
Little is known of this box, except the following from old railway workers. Wooden, shed-like structure. Painted whitish-grey. Size of a platelayers' hut. Signal lever bay underneath. Hand-pulled levers. Windows both sides, although Driver Jolly maintains Wivenhoe-facing side only.

Brightlingsea Station Signal Box (2)
Opened 3rd September, 1900: closed 30th October, 1922.
11'6" x 18'0" x ? Wood on brick construction
Signalman's floor 10 feet above rail level (verbal information)
Frame unknown 22 levers: 14 working; 8 spare

Wivenhoe Signal box abolished on 23rd July, 1967. The photograph was taken during better times in July, 1960. (*Photo Roger Kingstone*)

ACKNOWLEDGEMENTS

My thanks to all those people who, during the past twenty years, have helped me in so many ways, to make this book possible.